MW01098836

BRAVE,
MAD &
MEMORABLE

ROB HARLEY
JOURNALIST ON ASSIGNMENT

BRAVE,
MAD &
MEMORABLE

HarperCollins*Publishers*

For Brett Cammell and Linda Gollan
Thanks for sharing in the storytelling

National Library of New Zealand Cataloguing-in-Publication Data

Harley, Rob.
Brave, mad & memorable : journalist on assignment / Rob Harley.
ISBN 1-86950-444-5
1. Harley, Rob. 2. Television feature stories. 3. Reporters and reporting—
New Zealand. I. Title.
070.44—dc 21

First published 2002
Reprinted 2010
HarperCollins*Publishers (New Zealand) Limited*
P.O. Box 1, Auckland

ISBN 978 1 86950 444 1
Set in Plantin
Typeset by Chris O'Brien

CONTENTS

INTRODUCTION

Journalists are a privileged bunch. We get to dive into the middle of the lives of fascinating people, often when they're experiencing the most dramatic times of their existence. I've been writing now for nearly 29 years, and I never tire of the process of exploring lives in all their complexity. You can cover 'issues' till the cows come home — but there's nothing like a 'people' story.

Brave, Mad & Memorable is a collection of ten slices of my life — slices from my journalistic encounters with amazing people around the world. In most cases, the experiences I had with these people ended up forming part of TV documentaries. Approximately half of the tales come from my time on TVNZ current affairs programmes like *Frontline* and *Assignment*. The remainder are from a series called *Extreme Close Up* — a collection of stories that focused specifically on the role of faith and courage in the lives of ordinary people. *Extreme Close Up* was, for me, a master class in the study of human resilience.

Some people, like Kate Dominikovich, who battled on as a young mum after her husband's suicide, and Alan Routley, who scoured India to try to find his missing daughter, are heroes — the brave ones. There's another bunch, including Survivalist author and self-appointed high priest of the loony, Kurt Saxon ('The Poor Man's James Bond'), a man regarded by many in American law enforcement as both mad and bad.

Others are downright memorable, no two ways about it. Live for a while in the company of a young woman like Lee Savill, who lost all memory of her medical career and her marriage after a car crash, and you find out some powerful truths about courage. Journey a bit with a man like David Green, who battled to learn to walk again after his terrible injuries in the Ansett Dash 8 crash, and you get some major life lessons in forgiveness and guts.

The stories in this book are the reason I have never once woken up for work in this job and not looked forward to the day ahead. I'm very lucky. I trust that as you soak up a little of what I've learned from the brave, mad and memorable people I've met, you'll be inspired, smile a little, and maybe learn something along the way.

R.H.

1

SEARCHING FOR DIANA

The girl in the photo I'd been handed looked utterly charming.

Mid-twenties, I was picking — with a heart-melting smile and eyes that twinkled. If wholesomeness was still fashionable, this kid had it in spades. On appearances alone, the kind of young woman any mother would like her son to grow up and marry. Her name was Diana.

Diana Routley became a profound part of my life in the late 1990s. Her aunt called me one day, very concerned, to ask whether I could help her brother, Diana's dad, with some information about how to get people out of the clutches of weird religious cults.

I understood a little about this subject from previous journalistic encounters. Several New Zealanders I knew had been plucked from such organisations — usually in far-off places — and 'deprogrammed', after which they were eventually returned to their families.

Diana's aunt, Kath, said the young woman had gone missing on a backpacking holiday in India, and her family had heard nothing for several months. Her father, Alan, was now becoming so desperate for information he was willing to try anything, including exploring the possibility that Diana had been waylaid by some mystical experience in India from which she might be unable to escape.

My curiosity aroused, I spent some time talking with Alan and found myself in the company of a very loving father who was beside himself with worry about what might have happened to his 26-year-old girl. I was ultimately to go on a journey with Alan that would teach me an enormous amount about gaining perspective on life, and about how far a dad will go to try to rescue one of his children.

Photographs and videotapes have an almost painful poignancy when they're brought out to help show someone what a missing person looks like. Watching the many images I was offered, I realised Diana Routley was one of those free spirits who it is a delight to be around. In every family photograph she had either a quirky smile or a goofy look, or had been snapped at an airport coming or going on one of her working holidays.

Like many young New Zealanders, she headed for Britain and Europe in her early twenties and then undertook long, adventurous journeys to places like Africa. There she was, in one photo, with Table Mountain, in Cape Town, behind her. Journey's end for that moment — although just another way station in what Diana evidently hoped would be a very full life.

Basing herself in London, Diana had planned, in 1997, to take a leisurely overland route back to New Zealand via India. Best friend Tina Fleet recalls: 'She had this thing about India. She just had to go, there was no stopping her.' Perhaps it was her determination to retrace her father's travels to the subcontinent in the late 1950s. Whatever the motivation, Diana was not to be deterred, even when she couldn't find a travelling companion.

Several of her friends, and her dad, Alan, made Diana aware of their feelings about her going to India alone. They knew she was confident and careful, but the idea of her backpacking through that country by herself made many people apprehensive. Around this time there were several stories in the international media about young Westerners who had disappeared without trace on the subcontinent.

The assertive young Aucklander made a bit of a joke of everyone's concerns, and even wrote to a friend, Heather Frame, admitting openly that she knew how anxious her father was becoming about her intended journey. Writing to Heather in mid-1997, she confided: 'Get this, my dad is becoming more and more

10

paranoid, wants me to ring him every week.' But no one's caution or furrowed brow was going to make the Kiwi girl change her plans.

On 31 July 1997, a British Airways Boeing 747 left Heathrow, bound for New Delhi. Diana Routley was on her way to India. Like thousands of other backpackers on a limited budget, Diana made her way into the crowded bazaars of downtown New Delhi, to a place they call the Paharganj. Here, travellers from all over the world rub shoulders with Indian shopkeepers and eager young hustlers who try to part unwary sojourners from their cash.

In a cheap doss house called the Hotel Anup, the records show, Diana Routley spent several nights among newly arrived travellers from Britain, Germany and the Netherlands. The Paharganj would have given Diana a taste of India, both rich and risky. Here, they warn you not to take tea from strangers, as a naïve backpacker can easily be drugged and wake up minus passport and money.

After drinking in the sights and sounds of Delhi, Diana ventured south to Agra, home of the famed Taj Mahal. By this time she'd made friends with a couple of backpackers from England — Nick Baker and Lucy Manning — but was still essentially travelling alone. She was becoming entranced by India's awesome contrasts — great landmarks on the one hand, appalling poverty and need on the other. But there was nothing in her letters home that indicated she felt anything but safe and confident about her unfolding adventure.

From Agra it was south to Varanasi, India's holy city — the ancient place on the banks of the River Ganges where Hindu pilgrims come to bathe, pray, swim and die. Varanasi is an assault on the senses, filled with images stark and bizarre. Devout Hindus believe that if they die in Varanasi and then have their bodies burned on one of the funeral *ghats* that line the Ganges, they cease the relentless cycle of earthly struggle and go straight to heaven. If you're not wealthy enough to afford a funeral pyre, people may take kindly to your corpse, wrap it in muslin and drop it into the river.

It was very hot when Diana arrived in Varanasi on the train from Agra — the mercury was nudging 39 degrees. To keep faith with her dad, she rang home, informing Alan that her next stop would probably be Nepal. She sounded tired but chatty on the phone, and said she was looking forward to getting away from the heat of India and into the cool of the mountains.

Diana sought out cheap accommodation not far from the Ganges. She ended up at the Old Vishnu Guesthouse — although, as Alan Routley was later to learn, this was not the place she'd originally intended staying at, and the consequences would be ominous.

The Old Vishnu Guesthouse is down the end of a narrow lane filled with smells both alluring and repugnant. Diana had evidently kept her sense of humour, even in less-than-ideal digs, and wrote home: 'Since the shower/toilet is very small, I am not sure how I am supposed to have a shower without getting everything wet. So at the moment I fear that I might be a bit smelly!'

The Vishnu became Diana's base for exploring the ancient city, its markets, silk shops and stunning sights — tens of thousands of pilgrims standing in the muddy water undertaking a quirky series of daily rituals, some daubing themselves with mud, some brushing what few betel-stained teeth they possessed, others praying and splashing, and a few breathing their last and dying.

Diana's last contact with home was the phone call she made on 8 August 1997, telling Alan about the next stage of her journey. Back home in the Auckland suburb of Kohimarama, Alan and his wife, Shirley, were relieved to hear Diana was still safe and well, but they retained a sense of unease about her continued solitary travels. Their fears were to prove well founded, because that phone call in early August was to be followed by a long silence. After two or three weeks had passed, Alan became seriously concerned at not having heard from Diana.

He contacted Diana's cousin, Jane Culpan, in London, and she likewise reported that contact had dried up. 'That was completely unlike Diana,' said Jane. 'She was pretty good about letting many of us know what she was up to, and she'd given nobody any hint that she had any intention other than to make her way through India and Asia before arriving back in New Zealand. No plans to drop out or anything like that.'

In Wellington, the police were contacted and Interpol opened a file on Diana. Interpol officer Michelle Moore told the family they were right to be concerned, and said the sudden ending of communication from Diana was of grave concern, given she'd previously been so fastidious about making phone calls and sending letters.

In New Delhi, the New Zealand High Commission started making exhaustive checks. This wasn't the first time Kiwi diplomats in India had gone searching for a missing compatriot. India, it transpires, has an almost bewitching effect on some travellers. A few become so captivated by the country's attractions (including its potent varieties of weed) they grow lax over their usual routines of calling and writing home. Tales of young Kiwis turning up, starry-eyed, after a month or so in the company of an Indian holy man are not uncommon.

However, Diana's disappearance was treated seriously right from the outset. The High Commissioner to India, Adrian Simcock, made arrangements to go to Varanasi personally to liaise with local police. The Second Secretary at the High Commission, Priscilla Clark, started wandering through the alleys of the Paharganj to see if anyone had information about the missing Kiwi. This was the high season for Westerners visiting India, so hers was no small task.

In Katmandu, Nepal, the Honorary New Zealand Consul trekked round dozens of guesthouses, trying to determine if Diana had made it into the country. But no one had seen her. Months went by. As I talked over the process of waiting and wondering with Alan, I couldn't begin to imagine how tough it must have been as each day passed with no word from his daughter.

On Christmas Eve 1997, New Zealand High Commission staff waited anxiously at New Delhi's Indira Gandhi Airport to see if, by some faint chance, Diana would turn up to catch her booked flight back to London. They scanned the faces of the backpackers, but of Diana Routley there was no sign. Priscilla Clark called Alan Routley in Auckland the following morning. She says it was one of the hardest phone calls she's ever had to make.

It was early in 1998 that Alan's sister contacted me through TVNZ's *Assignment* programme, seeking help with information about cults in Asia, and any intelligence I might have of how people had managed to get relatives out of their clutches. In talking to Alan later, it struck me this was a fairly vain attempt to get any answer at all to the question of where Diana might have ended up.

'It's about all I can think of now,' said Alan wearily. 'Perhaps she got in with the wrong crowd, got brainwashed, and has become too disoriented to call us. I guess at the moment I don't want to even contemplate alternative explanations for not hearing from her.'

There'd still been no contact, and communication between New Zealand and central India was difficult, to say the least. I vividly remember sitting in Alan's lounge one evening as the meticulous father showed me the bulging file he had assembled. Diana's cheery face shone out from a dozen blown-up photos filed among the faxes and correspondence from far-off places.

By April, Alan had made up his mind. He told his two other children, Matthew and Helen, he would spend every cent he owned — and he was relatively well-off — including whatever might otherwise come their way in the form of an inheritance, to exhaust all possibilities in the search for Diana. No one put up any objection. To start with, he intended to go to India personally. This struck me as a very bold — some would say risky — move for a man in his sixties. India was completely foreign territory, and Alan was to learn that the disappearance of Westerners in this land of more than a billion people was not uncommon.

The semiretired civil engineer had hundreds of posters printed in both English and Hindi — bright-yellow ones — with a smiling picture of Diana and words pleading for information as to her whereabouts. He arranged to meet Matthew, flying in from America, in New Delhi, and then the two of them would do whatever it took. They'd search Varanasi and anywhere else it seemed at all likely Diana would be.

It was an emotional time at Auckland airport as Alan said goodbye to Shirley, Helen and the grandchildren. Wiping away tears, Helen told me: 'She could be anywhere. I'm kind of hoping she's been mugged, and she's missing her pack and traveller's cheques and she's stuck somewhere in the Indian outback and can't contact us. I hope, I just hope.'

Alan was typically straightforward. 'I don't know what we're going to find,' he said. 'In fact, we may not even find anything, but I've got to give it my best shot.' This was a man with a fine and logical mind — an engineering expert who'd been doing major work at the Lake Manapouri power station, deep in the South Island, only a couple of weeks before. He was about to apply that analytical brain to the most emotionally challenging task of his life.

By the end of only his first week in India, Alan had managed to establish something had clearly gone very wrong for his girl. Having found the guest lodge in Varanasi where she'd stayed, he discovered, in the company of Indian police, that there were staff there who remembered Diana quite vividly. His amateur detective work uncovered a man who'd taken Diana and two English tourists for a boat trip on the Ganges on the morning of 8 August — the very day she'd called home for the last time. From this encounter he began to unravel more threads.

Alan put up a poster at the guesthouse, as in so many other places, asking for help. He saw where Diana had spent the last night anyone was able to account for. It was a stark concrete room with a simple bed and a large cooling fan whirring away overhead.

Then, on the roof of the Old Vishnu Guesthouse, Alan finally spoke to some people who were able to put the first real pieces of the puzzle together for him. He learned about a man called Dharam Deva Yadav — a self-styled Don Juan — who'd stayed at the guesthouse and made a nuisance of himself with several Western women over the previous year.

Yadav had been seen with Diana two days after she'd last called home. At precisely the time Diana had last been seen in Varanasi, Yadav had himself disappeared for an extended period of time. Alan started to get a gnawing feeling in the pit of his stomach. All the information he was gathering suggested Diana had been enticed by Yadav to visit his home village, called Brindivan, about 70 kilometres north of Varanasi.

The Indian police were starting to take notice. After doing some crosschecking of their own, the police told Alan they considered Yadav a strong suspect in Diana's disappearance, and were especially interested in reports that he'd worked hard in the past at trying to seduce other Western women travellers.

It would emerge later that Diana had intended to go to Darjeeling, and then on to Nepal, but that Yadav had convinced her to change her plans — showing her photos of other foreign women who had visited his village — and then cancel her tickets to Darjeeling. Yadav, a man of consummate persistence and persuasion, then helped Diana buy new tickets to Brindivan. Alan could barely believe what he was uncovering.

While Alan was still in Varanasi, police raided Yadav's home, but he'd been tipped off and had fled. Evidently he had a network of friends and contacts all over the country, and he would prove to be highly elusive. How had a savvy Kiwi woman traveller, who presumably had had her share of unwelcome attention while on the road, been lured into what now smelled like such serious trouble?

As Alan pursued his enquiries in Varanasi, he discovered a tragic truth about Diana's arrival in the town. It turned out she'd got off the train from Agra and had asked to be taken to a guesthouse that had been recommended to her. However, as often happens with wide-eyed Western travellers, Diana had ended up in the company of a rickshaw driver who was looking for a few easy rupees and had taken her to a different place — the Old Vishnu Guesthouse — no doubt earning himself a kickback in the process. Probably tired and full of resignation after a long, hot journey, Diana, Alan could well imagine, had simply decided she'd stay where she'd been dropped off.

The tragic part of this was that the guesthouse where she'd been taken was the haunt of a man who regarded young, attractive Western women as easy prey. Tales of Yadav's persistent advances to women travellers started to emerge in more detail as Alan kept asking around.

But the trail had gone well and truly cold. The police were making no progress at all.

When Alan finally felt he'd run out of options, he came back to New Zealand, wondering what to do next. 'The police there tried to be helpful, but you have to understand how slowly things move in that country,' Alan told me wearily. 'I think I'll go back, but I want to gather my thoughts before I make my next journey.'

About three months later I was due to go to England for a conference, and with Alan planning his second journey to Varanasi, I decided to take a punt and accompany him for part of the trip.

It was clearly going to be quite a challenge. The best advice I got was that I'd probably get nowhere if I arrived with a full camera crew. So I decided to teach myself how to use one of the new high-quality digital video cameras coming onto the market, and after a week or so I felt sufficiently confident to go to India on my own to find Alan and document the next stage of his search for Diana.

After a couple of days' travelling, I walked off the plane at Varanasi airport into a sweltering 40 degrees and a breaking thunderstorm. Alan met me and we drove into the heart of Varanasi through a huge downpour, water lapping through the floorboards of the ancient Morris Oxford cab. (These cars are everywhere in India, where they are still manufactured.)

As I pulled one of the video cameras out of my bag to begin taping, I felt a sense of dread as I looked into the viewfinder. The camera had completely seized up in the humidity and was refusing to take any pictures. Second camera — same story. My heart sank, and I felt like a helpless amateur. How was I going to justify coming all the way here at great expense only to return home with no pictures?

But Alan was very patient. I checked into the $US30-a-night Diamond Hotel where he was staying and we waited it out, hoping the cameras would adjust to the oppressive, moist atmosphere. After about an hour they did (be still my beating heart!), and Alan and I launched into documenting what he hoped would be some serious progress in his attempts to find Diana.

Varanasi, I was informed by a nearly toothless rickshaw driver who befriended me, is one of the most ancient continuously inhabited cities in the world. I spent fascinating hours on the back of his rattly contraption as he hauled me through the streets of the city, spitting ghastly lumps of betel-nut juice into the gutters as he pedalled. This was only my second trip to Asia — the first had been two weeks in Vietnam eight years earlier. I found myself utterly captivated by the smells and sights of the chaotic crush of humanity around me.

My rickshaw driver waited for me as I filmed at the Varanasi railway station, trying to capture a sense of what Diana Routley must have experienced as she arrived in that mad place, where sacred cattle mix with desperate, leprous beggars whose bodies swarm with flies. I tried to imagine Diana disembarking, and could well understand how she might have been only to eager to take the first ride on offer.

The scenes on the River Ganges were even more eye-catching. The riverbank plays host to what appears to be a continuous festival of death and dedication — corpses drift slowly by, while only metres away in the putrid water, pilgrims pray, wash and clean their teeth. It's like some kind of mad theatre of the absurd, wreathed in the smoke that billows ceaselessly from the funeral pyres fed by a never-ending supply of timber ferried down the Ganges on creaking barges. It was OK to use a camera most of the time, I was told, except when a funeral pyre was lit. I figured my story could probably manage without burning corpses, anyway.

Alan had teamed up with a helpful local businessman, who insisted on anonymity but had an excellent intelligence network; his antennae were well tuned for information about people like Dharam Deva Yadav. By now he and Alan had managed to establish that Yadav was an extremely manipulative man. Word was out that he'd taken several Western women backpackers to Brindivan, and that one of them, an Austrian, had become sufficiently spellbound by him to be still sending him money.

Yadav, it transpired, had a family, but moved about in a somewhat shadowy fashion, working in guesthouses like the Old Vishnu in Varanasi and trying his charms on foreign females as an illegal tour guide. I followed Alan as he tramped through the back alleys of Varanasi trying to establish some kind of chain of events leading up to Diana's disappearance. The streets and lanes at that time of year were full of fresh-faced European tourists being driven on rickshaws to who knew where.

Alan found a shop where Diana, according to the large record book Indian shopkeepers are fond of keeping, had bought silk just a couple of days before she'd disappeared. Had anyone taken much notice of whom she was with, Alan wanted to know? The details of Diana's purchases were meticulously recorded, but no one seemed to be able to remember with any clarity whether Yadav, whose picture Alan was now carrying with him, had been in Diana's company.

Alan was becoming increasingly anxious and frustrated. His own relentless questioning, he hoped, would goad the Indian police into being more vigorous with their enquiries. The case appeared to have stalled — cops were being moved to other jobs. It was a constant three-steps-forward, two-steps-back kind of shuffle.

'I think it's quite absurd,' Alan told me one afternoon as we sat in his hotel room. 'There's clear evidence Yadav was involved in Diana's disappearance, yet there seems to be a great slowness about tracking him down and asking him the right questions. I find it quite incomprehensible that a man who's known to have molested people and extorted money from them, with the obvious complicity of others in his village, is allowed to escape questioning.'

By now another major clue had come Alan's way. It had emerged that $3,000 of Diana's traveller's cheques had been cashed in the Indian city of Jaipur in September, a month after her disappearance. Jaipur was known to be another of Yadav's favourite haunts.

My videotape from that afternoon's conversation shows a very worn-out Kiwi dad, with deep lines on his face, looking with sadness and resignation out of the window of the Diamond Hotel. How could I identify with Alan's kind of pain? My little girl, Kate, was six years old at the time — losing her was simply too much to contemplate. We were rapidly approaching the one-year anniversary of Diana's disappearance.

Eventually Alan shrugged and said: 'I've found from long experience that at times like this you've got to get on and do something. Maybe it's a kind of placebo effect; at least you feel like you're having a go.' The bills were starting to mount up — tens of thousands of dollars in travel expenses and phone calls. But there were no plans to quit.

Dealing with the local police was something of a mixed bag. There was one particular officer, Subinspector Raghavendra Singh, whom Alan felt was taking the case very seriously, but sometimes the advice he received from other senior police officers in the district was quite disturbing. One police chief he and I interviewed together — an apparently sane and rational man — suggested Alan bring an article of Diana's clothing for an Indian holy man to smell, and he would be able to tell from the odour of the garment whether she was dead or alive.

As the chief gave this advice, I must admit my eyes bulged a little. But Alan simply nodded and gave me the clear impression he'd be prepared to try just about anything. By this stage, it emerged, Alan had also sought the advice of clairvoyants and psychics, but their counsel had produced no consistent theme or answer. One clairvoyant had told him she'd seen Diana in a vision beside a river. She'd been injured, said the woman; she'd been hit on the head and was distressed.

'The clairvoyant was not very hopeful about us finding Diana in good condition if we find her at all,' said Alan. 'Whereas last time when I came here the police were all telling me we would find her, and that she would be alive, they're not telling me that any more. The senior policemen I'm speaking to are all warning me that there's not a very big chance of finding her alive after one year.'

After four days in Varanasi, I prepared to leave Alan for New Delhi, to complete filming in the Indian capital with embassy people and the like. It was a fairly wistful goodbye at Varanasi airport; I had come to like and admire this man who was working so hard in the face of such long odds. We'd become friends, and I sensed he was going to miss my company as he prepared to begin another round of banging on doors trying to rustle up some action.

I filmed interviews in New Delhi with the New Zealand High Commissioner, and picked up a range of illustrative material around the city, and then further south, in Agra, around the Taj Mahal. It was easy to see why young people such as Diana find India a beautiful and captivating place to visit. I spent a day wandering through the Paharganj, watching a host of young Western tourists, trying to picture in my mind the innocent enthusiasm that Diana had probably brought to her sojourn there.

Then, in England, I sought out another grieving dad, in Wiltshire — Frank Mogford, who'd lost his son, Ian, in India two years previously. Same story as Diana — a sudden end to all communication, then trips by Frank to India in search of his boy, but to no avail. Frank Mogford and Alan Routley were, I learned, part of a sad international fraternity.

Meanwhile, back in India, the next stage of Alan's investigation was turning out to be like something from a thriller novel. With his anonymous business contact in Varanasi, Alan set a trap for Yadav. They sent word to Yadav by a roundabout route that there was money waiting for him at a hotel in Bombay. Alan figured Yadav would come out of hiding if he thought there were rupees in it for him.

Alan posed as an Austrian medical rep called Sep Lukas. Yadav didn't turn up in Bombay, but a few days later took the bait for a rendezvous with 'Herr Lukas' at a hotel back in Varanasi. With Subinspector Singh hiding in Alan's hotel bathroom, the set-up was in place. It was an incredible moment. Yadav knocked at the door of Alan's room, and suddenly the dad from Auckland was face to face with the man he was sure had abducted his daughter.

Within moments, Singh was out of the bathroom, blocking Yadav's escape, and they were unfurling one of the posters with Diana's face on to thrust under Yadav's nose. Sensing the game was up, Yadav made up an elaborate tale about Diana having gone to stay with a friend's brother in Katmandu. Over the next few days, the police questioned Yadav and one of his associates exhaustively, and agreed to a one-on-one session between Alan and the Indian man.

Alan recalls: 'People have asked me how I felt being in his presence. I think there was that tiny shred of hope in me that Diana may indeed have still been alive — perhaps off in a commune somewhere, maybe living with a guy in either India or Nepal. Yadav kept telling me stories which kept that hope alive.'

While Alan went to Katmandu with Subinspector Singh to check Yadav's story, police back in Varanasi took Yadav to a local temple and tried one last tactic. They asked him to swear by a sacred Indian deity that Diana was still alive. At about the time Alan was concluding the Katmandu story was a lie, Yadav cracked and told the police the truth.

I got back to New Zealand, and about a week later came the phone call from Alan that I'd been half expecting but dreading nonetheless. His deep voice laden with sadness, Alan told me on the line from Varanasi that the police had arrested four men, including Yadav. The men, all of them from Brindivan, had confessed to having committed an awful crime.

Without knowing the full story Alan was taken on a journey by car and boat to the small village. A tall, gaunt, white-headed figure among the smaller, swarthy Indians, Alan Routley had been led to

Yadav's home and ushered with decorum into a small room with an earthen floor. Finally, he learnt the truth. Yadav had confessed to the police that he and his three friends had attacked Diana in his home.

In his subsequent statement, Yadav would admit that his intentions towards Diana had been evil right from the start. Having got the young New Zealander into his home, he had sent his family away to stay with relatives on some pretext before setting out to rape and rob Diana.

When she'd put up a fight and threatened to go to the police, Yadav's companions had held her, and Yadav had strangled her with a scarf.

It had been brutal, cold and calculated. They'd hatched a plan to sell Diana's traveller's cheques on the black market, then buried her body under the floor of Yadav's house. By the time Alan got to Brindivan, all there was to see was a hole in a dark, wretched room and the carefully arranged skeletal remains of his beloved daughter.

I found myself breathing heavily, almost gasping, as I listened to Alan recount the events from so many kilometres away. Finally, there was a sense of resignation in his voice, tempered with something that I was able to identify only a little bit later — the tiniest bit of consolation that at last he knew what had befallen Diana.

We had intended taking considerable time and care over editing the documentary, but now we had a development that meant we'd have to produce our story much more quickly.

While I worked with editor John Otimi and producer John Gillespie, frantically compressing a two-week edit into four days, researcher Jane Skinner raced around town conducting the last few interviews. *Assignment* production manager Penelope Thomas and producer Trish Carter did a ton of international negotiating. They arranged for Alan's friend, the businessman from Varanasi (a restaurateur, it transpired), to drive the 36 hours from Varanasi to Delhi in an old Morris Oxford with a videotape taken by a local TV channel recording the scene that had greeted Alan in Brindivan. Penelope conducted a long-distance chess game, managing to get people and tapes through embassies and into TV satellite stations just in time to be included in our edit.

When the grainy footage finally came through over the satellite, I felt an enormous lump in my throat as I watched this man who'd become quite a dear friend standing silently at the edge of what had been his daughter's grave for more than a year.

Journey's end.

The Indian TV crew had recorded a host of images that day. Alan said it was fine to use all of the pictures except one. This was an official police photograph, for which Yadav and his three co-offenders had been forced to line up with the remains of Diana Routley, curled in a foetal position, at their feet.

The image, when it came across the satellite, was, mercifully, very blurred — just a bundle, it seemed, with some long hair protruding from one end.

A hundred questions flood your mind at a time like that. Who else in the village must have known? Surely Yadav's wife must have been aware of something afoot? What kind of man lives with such an awful secret in his own home?

As we were putting the finishing touches to our documentary, which we entitled *Innocents Abroad*, Alan, from India, was undertaking painful but necessary telephone conferences with Interpol officers in Wellington, arranging for medical and dental records to be sent over so the identity of the remains could be confirmed. Ultimately, there was no doubt.

Our eventual programme not only examined Diana's fate but also explored the anguish caused by the disappearance of several other Western tourists in India over the previous three years. Interviews we conducted in Australia and England showed that the pain of uncertainty for relatives of other young people who'd simply vanished was as palpable as that experienced by Alan and Shirley Routley and their family.

'I don't hate India,' Diana's sister, Helen, told me in her final interview for *Assignment*. We reflected, as we spoke, that over recent years several young tourists in New Zealand had suffered violent death at the hands of evil people. 'It wasn't a country that did this to my sister, it was four greedy men. It could have happened anywhere.'

Alan arranged to have Diana's remains cremated in Varanasi then brought back to New Zealand. The small urn arrived home a few days after a memorial service had been held. At a church near the Auckland waterfront where Diana had grown up, friends from school sang a tribute to their lost friend — 'Top of the World', the 1973 Carpenters' hit.

Whatever limited satisfaction the Routleys now felt about the fact that the men who'd killed Diana were going to be brought to justice was to be relatively short-lived. The Indian legal process is incredibly cumbersome, and as the months went by it became clear there would be no swift resolution.

Murder trials in India, it transpires, can go on for years. Some-times proceedings are held up for months at a time because of the unavailability of some witnesses due to farming schedules and the like. Some two-and-a-half years after the arrest of Yadav and his companions, Alan Routley was still waiting for the court to make any material progress in trying the men. In desperation, he asked New Zealand's foreign affairs minister, Phil Goff, to intervene on the family's behalf during an official visit to India.

Goff pressed the case with Indian authorities, and soon after-wards Alan was asked to go to India to give evidence at the trial. However, by this time Alan was approaching 70 years of age and his health had taken a turn for the worse. 'I don't think you can go through something like this without it taking a serious toll on you,' he told me recently. 'I think it's knocked me around more than I had imagined.'

As I pondered the case, I thought to myself it would be a shame if people got the idea that travel to places like India is inherently dangerous. But it made me realise, as I looked at my own daugh-ter, how energetically I would try to dissuade her, as Alan obviously did with Diana, from undertaking solo travel in any part of the world. Life is simply too precious.

Alan Routley taught me some big lessons about persistence and sheer devotion to family. There was nothing he would not have spent or given away had he felt Diana might yet be alive and able to be rescued, and he also evidently thought he'd have gone on spend-ing and looking until he'd found Diana in whatever condition she might have been. I guess I would like to think there's someone who loves me enough — who cares for me as much as Alan did for Diana — to go looking for me if I ever drop out of sight.

UPDATE

As this book went to print, all four men accused of Diana Routley's murder were out on bail. The trial seems to have ground to a halt — again. The prosecution had indicated it intended calling 70 witnesses. By early 2002, the court had heard from only nine. There have now been four prosecutors. Each, in succession, has been moved on to other duties. The latest one, a woman, doesn't speak very good English, and Alan has great difficulty understanding what's going on. Sometimes he gets an Indian friend to come to his home, and they get on the phone together to try to make sense of what's going on in Varanasi.

An 85-page document Alan has been sent, which includes details of the evidence he might give by affidavit, contains a number of factual errors. This is distressing, to say the least. Alan has estimated the cost of a further trip to Varanasi to help set things right at over $30,000. He's decided neither his health nor his bank balance will stand another passage to India.

2

THE POOR MAN'S JAMES BOND

On 13 November 1990, New Zealand entered a club that no nation ever wants to join. Into the record books was entered the name of a disturbed young man called David Gray, who one afternoon flew into a dark rage, took up firearms and went on a several-hour killing spree. It happened in a tiny seaside settlement called Aramoana, in the South Island.

Gray shot to death 13 of his neighbours, including small children and a brave local policeman, Sergeant Stu Guthrie, who tried to get Gray to lay down his weapons. He set fire to a house, then roamed through the neighbourhood all night, brandishing high-calibre guns, while a massive security operation was launched to try to capture him.

The carnage was finally ended when policemen from the Armed Offenders Squad cornered Gray in the by-then deserted settlement and shot him. The TV news pictures that evening showed long-range images of tear gas and black-clad warriors accompanied by the crackle of automatic weapons. It felt to us all like something from another land. It was our worst mass murder.

In the inevitable and wide-ranging analyses that followed that terrible 22 hours in Aramoana, a huge number of questions were asked and explanations offered. It was quite clear that Gray, over a period of several years, had been steadily deteriorating into a mad and bitter person, gathering guns and soaking himself in paranoia and hate. Much of the ensuing discussion was about New Zealand's firearms laws and the kinds of deadly weapons that can fall into the hands of psychotic individuals.

I was working on other documentary projects at the time, and didn't get involved in reporting the issues until several months later. The story I ultimately came to tell was, in its own way, just as chilling as the first reports to emerge from the tiny shattered community.

Journalist Kelvin Dick, from Wellington, had come to us at TVNZ with some fairly compelling research he'd done on Aramoana. It turned out that Gray, as his mind had slowly slipped away, had been feeding himself on a steady diet of what policemen call mayhem literature — books and magazines glorifying the use of guns and explosives. It was the presence of large amounts of this kind of writing in Gray's house that really disturbed New Zealand's head police psychologist, Dr Ian Miller.

'His home was full of the stuff,' Miller told us. 'As the guy slowly veered towards lunacy, he was ingesting copious quantities of this poisonous material.'

One mayhem author in particular, it seemed, had been a particularly strong influence on Gray: Kurt Saxon, a lonely and embittered writer, who hailed from a small town called Harrison in the American state of Arkansas. Saxon, the son of a bankrupted peanut farmer from Wichita, Kansas, was the notorious author of such books as *The Poor Man's James Bond* — a very nasty volume detailing various methods of poisoning, blowing up and shooting others.

Quite early in my research I got to see one of Saxon's strange videos, which could be ordered through the mail. It included detailed instructions on how to make a time-release bomb with common chemicals, which, when placed in a small plastic jar and dropped into a car's fuel tank, would eventually cause a deadly explosion. Saxon presents the video from behind a desk in his basement, wearing a trilby decorated with a feather. The hands of the grizzled anarchist are clearly marred — lost fingers from his own less-than-successful experiments.

Although the entire concept sounds horrifying, free-speech provisions in the American Constitution permit the writing and distribution of this stuff. Remember, all this was going on well before the age of the Internet. Saxon's vitriolic material was relatively well known around the world, and actively sought out by disaffected and disturbed people.

As well as finding some of Saxon's material in Gray's home, Miller came across some letters — correspondence between Gray in Aramoana and Saxon in Harrison. Gray had written to Saxon asking for advice on ammunition and guns for 'defensive purposes'. The letters showed Saxon had responded readily, advising a certain type of bullet was 'what Gray needed'.

From even our preliminary conversations with law enforcement officials in the United States, it became clear the kind of advice Saxon had given Gray was typical of information he was in the habit of providing to disenfranchised and angry young men all over the world.

At the time I was working for a TVNZ current affairs programme called *Frontline,* and since there'd been no major television examination of what had happened at Aramoana, we felt, in the January following the massacre, it was high time we explored some of the factors behind the awful events that had devastated the small South Island community.

As Miller told us: 'While Kurt Saxon may not actually have been in Aramoana pulling the trigger, he exerted such a powerful influence over David Gray that he might as well have been there, taking part in the mayhem.'

To some people, reaching that conclusion might have seemed to be drawing rather a long bow, but in any event we thought it would be valuable at least to see whether we could get underneath the skin of the Arkansas guru of American Survivalists (a term and concept I'll explore in a moment). Kelvin Dick planned to come with us to America to collect material for a book on the Survivalist phenomenon.

One morning we called Saxon at his Arkansas home from our office in Auckland. I don't quite know what we were expecting, but I was a little apprehensive — speaking to someone who had boastfully owned up to having been involved in a number of killings himself. The voice on the other end of the phone, with a deep Southern drawl, was that of a man who was disarmingly genial and invited us to 'come on over'. Saxon said he'd be prepared to answer any question we felt appropriate to put to him.

It was to be for us a disturbing journey into the heartland of American Survivalism and right-wing mania, and a full-on revelation of what can happen to the human heart when you expose it to enough hatred and paranoia. The term 'Survivalist' is one, apparently, that Saxon boasted he had invented. It had come to refer to the looniest of the American loony right, who were heading for the hills and for armed compounds in the 1970s and 80s to escape taxes and government interference in their lives, and to prepare for the 'inevitability' of Soviet invasion. Saxon was one of their heroes — a man whose books and videos told them, and other mad loners, how to get ready for urban warfare. More on the Survivalists a little later.

So, off we went — to find Saxon, and to talk to those who had labelled him one of the most serious threats to internal stability yet to emerge in the United States. On the way, we collected videotape and interviews on a subject that was proving to be as troubling, in its own way, to Americans as to Kiwis.

Just wander through some of the heavy-duty surplus military hardware stores that proliferate throughout the USA, glance at a couple of the books that tell you how to hurt your fellow man in 101 new ways, marvel at all the fuse wire and practice grenades, and you're on a steep education curve.

The little town of Harrison, Arkansas, is around 100 kilometres south of the Missouri border, and it's about as deep South, backwoods Dixieland as you can get: 18 radio stations, 17 of them playing country and western; a rotund sheriff called Bucky; and a town square populated by grizzled old men spitting and whittling away aimlessly on pieces of wood. Fair in the middle of the square is a flagpole with an MIA (Missing In Action) flag, commemorating the soldiers still believed held in Vietnam, fluttering proudly next to the Confederate colours. The only places to eat, apparently, serve fried chicken and grits — a kind of greasy porridge that is a rite of passage for visitors with a stomach strong enough to face it.

As we drove into town we were stopped by a burly policeman, who, having held up our line of traffic, turned to perform a stiff salute to a hearse creeping slowly by towards the cemetery, followed by at least 50 cars. We were indeed in the South.

In a very modest house on a hill above this town of 8000 people, we found Kurt Saxon. You're not quite sure what you're going to get when you find the front door opened by a man with such a fearsome reputation, but he was shorter than we'd imagined, slightly pot-bellied, with greying hair and full of loud Southern hospitality and welcome.

And so it was, that day in early 1991, that we were introduced to the nightmarish world of a man who, by all accounts, had been the inspiration for many acts of terrorism around the world, not only in Aramoana. Saxon, it turned out, was a former mental hospital orderly whose thought processes, somewhere along the line, had gone off on a screwed-up sidetrack, to the point where he had come to devote his life to the instruction of others in the art of murder and mayhem.

From our conversations with him, it was clear Saxon had once believed that one day the Soviet Union would invade America. That day in his home, he introduced us to his 'product range', including videotapes, books and pamphlets, designed to titillate and provoke any of his fellow countrymen who felt like trying out his murderous techniques well in advance of the Russian arrival. In his front room there was a charming little device on the coffee table — a syringe filled with deadly poison, disguised as a cigarette lighter, ready to be stabbed into the leg of the first Soviet through the door. If that didn't work, there was a black blunderbuss behind the front door, with a blast 'guaranteed to stop an elephant'.

So we sat down in Saxon's lounge and began one of the most extraordinary interviews I have ever undertaken. I had a long list of questions about the outrageous hallmarks of Saxon's philosophy, which I wanted to cover with him before we got round to his relationship with New Zealand's worst mass killer.

One of Saxon's specialities is poisoning. In his manual *The Poor Man's James Bond*, he gives bald and frightening instructions on how to test out poison. The initial victim ought to be a homeless person or a 'wino', urges Saxon, because their lives count for so little anyway.

Quoting directly from the book:

Put the dose you want to test in a bottle of wine. Tuck it where the wino will be sure to find it. If the nest has a dead wino in it the next morning, you've figured out the right dose. If both the nest and the bottle are empty, it's back to the old drawing board.

You get no clue at any point in the book, or in your conversation with Saxon, that he is anything other than deadly serious. 'Try increasing the dosage', is his simple advice on perfecting your technique with your chosen poison. As we commenced our interview with Saxon, the setting belied the awfulness of the man and his mind. Reviewing the tape of the interview, one can see a line of cuddly teddy bears on a shelf behind Saxon's shoulder. Quaint homeliness in a mad place.

Saxon, his hair slicked back and moustache neatly trimmed, listened without a flicker as I asked him: 'So if someone read your book, followed this advice about poisoning and then acted on it, you'd consider that they had followed quite serious advice?'

'Well, I think that would be the best test of it,' Saxon told me. 'I mean I've known a lot of winos — I used to live at the Wino Arms in Long Beach, California. They're very miserable people, they have no reason for living, and if I could send them off to the happy land with a little dose of something in their wine, what better?'

It's one of those rare moments in journalism when the answer you've just been given is so outrageous and gobsmacking that you don't quite know what to do next. 'You're deadly serious about that?' I asked him.

'Oh sure, why not? I mean if I was a wino, living in the gutter, sleeping in little nests like that and someone helped me out, I'd thank him.'

And such was to be the tone of the rest of our encounter. I found myself torn as I listened to Saxon speaking in his calm and measured way: was this pure nonsense — black humour — or highly inflammatory and potentially deadly raving?

As the interview went on, I cast my mind back to some observations made only a few days earlier, when, in Washington, D.C., we'd visited Dr Neil Livingstone, an American expert on domestic and international terrorism. Livingstone has for years been an advisor to governments around the world on identifying and combating terrorist threats. He draws a clear link between the writings of individuals like Kurt Saxon and actual acts of mayhem.

He says where you find terrorism and mad behaviour, you all too often find the writings of mayhem authors underpinning them. 'This stuff is found in the homes of felons and criminals all over the United States,' Livingstone told me. 'You find it in the safe houses of domestic and international terrorism groups, and you have to assume that if this material — this advice on how to hurt others — is turning up over and over again, that it's having an influence on them or instructing them in some way.'

There are policemen in big American cities, like Chicago, who agree with this contention. After we'd picked Livingstone's brains and were heading towards Arkansas, we dropped in on Dave Ryan, from the Chicago Police Department's Violent Crime Unit. In a stark, squat building not far from the centre of town, you find Ryan amidst a stack of files detailing some of the most gruesome crimes imaginable. He talks to you in measured tones about tracking down multiple killers, who sometimes throw their victims into a lake just as winter's beginning, because they know it will freeze over and cover up their dastardly work until well into spring, when the thaw comes. But his voice has an edge of weariness, as if he has seen one too many awful things in his life and is now assailed by numbness.

Ryan's interest in Saxon and his ilk was quite specialised. In 1982, Ryan was trying to find the person who had been lacing bottles of Tylenol capsules in the Chicago area with a fatal poison. The poisoner had been doing his work with deadly precision. In September of that year, completely unsuspecting victims, like Paula Prince, bought Tylenol capsules at major pharmacies. Paula's last purchase was at a Walgreen's drugstore in downtown Chicago. From a box, Ryan calmly pulled a video cassette showing security camera pictures of Paula in the store, buying her capsules.

Less than half an hour after the pictures were taken, she was dead — a victim of a highly potent poison in the capsules she had innocently bought for a headache. She was one of seven who died from taking contaminated capsules. Although the Chicago police never formally charged anyone with the Tylenol killings, Ryan and his fellow officers were sure that a man who had once been a strong suspect in the case was the guilty one. Roger Arnold, arrested the following year for shooting dead a barman, had a home full of the apparatus and literature of murder when he was questioned about the Tylenol killings.

'He had a large number of firearms, pipe bombs and other similar material,' Ryan told me. 'We also found two books: *The Poor Man's James Bond* by Kurt Saxon and another one you often find in these places, called *The Anarchist's Cookbook*. Both of these explain various methods of poisoning people and building other devices for hurting your fellow man.'

The key question I had for Ryan was this: 'Was there enough information in Saxon's book about the manufacture and use of potassium cyanide to have given the Tylenol poisoner sufficient information to lace the capsules with their deadly load?'

'Without a doubt,' Ryan told me. 'Absolutely.'

The FBI, we learned, had questioned Saxon about the Tylenol case, and had asked for his mailing list to try to find the killer. In an edition of *The Poor Man's James Bond* written after the Tylenol killings, Saxon had added some new material. Again, it was breathtaking in its sheer cold-bloodedness.

'Anyone can murder anyone with my book,' Saxon wrote. 'And I endorse it, and I promote it.' He went on: 'I think if you have "The Poor Man's James Bond", you can kill anyone you want. That's a great thing.'

As I pressed him on his words that afternoon, Saxon, for once during our encounter, smiled and said that he'd been joking, and people should have understood the humour.

'So why give instructions in your book as to how to make and use potassium cyanide?' I asked him. 'Of what use is that to anyone, other than someone who is intent on doing harm to a fellow human being?'

'Well, if you wanted to do harm to a Russian — and I don't think the Russian threat is by any means over.' It's helpful to remember at this point, perhaps, that by now the Berlin wall had gone and the Soviet bloc was in tatters.

'So everything you've put there in *The Poor Man's James Bond* about explosives and poison — that's all there to counter the Russian threat?' I went on.

Saxon simply shrugged. 'Well, could be, but you've gotta re-member internal threats as well. I'm trying to help people get ready for those too.' Wherein, of course, you find the sinister implications of what Saxon counsels and teaches.

It's hard to know what internal threat Saxon might have had in mind when, in the late 1980s, schoolboys started copying in earnest the designs he gave in *The Poor Man's James Bond* for very danger-ous pipe bombs. These devices, able to be made in a home workshop, started wreaking havoc all over the United States, and the conse-quences were tying up hundreds of law enforcement officers, not to mention hospital staff and, often, funeral directors. Following up on some stories about pipe bomb mayhem, we went to see Sergeant Conrad Grayson from the San Diego Sheriff's Department. He showed us a chamber of horrors in his back room: pictures of muti-lated young men and a collection of bombs made from materials that schoolboys had got together, probably with nothing very sinis-ter in mind, but with consequences far from benign.

'Here's one,' said Grayson, holding up a hefty piece of pipe with nails taped to the side and a fuse protruding from one end. 'Some boys made another one just like this and when it didn't go off, they put it in the back of their car and drove home. The trou-ble is, halfway home the bomb went off, killing the driver.'

All across the display table were bits of shrapnel, which, Grayson said, had in many cases shredded flesh as they'd exploded and flown apart at 3200 miles per hour. The sad and disastrous conse-quences for boys, as young as 13, of packing chemicals inside pipes and then undertaking experiments: the loss of limbs, even their lives.

Surely the most sinister device on display in Grayson's office was something dubbed a book bomb. Pull back the cover on a large and worthy-looking hardback volume, and you discover a pipe bomb wired to a trigger. Simple concept — an unsuspecting reader opens the book and gets blinded, maimed or killed. What infuriates Grayson as we're talking to him is that when he looks at the designs of the bombs he recovers, he finds they are exact rep-licas of devices carefully detailed in books such as *The Poor Man's James Bond*. Indeed, when he lined up the devices he had on dis-play next to Saxon's designs, it was clear San Diego schoolboys had followed Saxon's instructions religiously, with sometimes deadly results.

Things that go together: bombs, books and blasted bodies. For Sergeant Grayson it is a constantly recurring scenario. 'I'm the one that has to go to the homes and inform these poor parents what has happened to their son and his friends. Kids have lost their fingers, been crippled or been killed, then you go into the bedrooms of these young guys, their mother in tears, and you discover almost inevitably on their bookshelves volumes like *The Anarchist's Cookbook* or *The Poor Man's James Bond*.'

The big question we'd come to ask, of course, was this: was there a link between the ravings and advice of Kurt Saxon and the meltdown of David Gray in Aramoana? Gray, an individual who'd shut himself off from previous friends and his neighbourhood, kept one line of communication open: correspondence with the writers of mayhem literature and gun magazines. It was clear he'd developed a passion for, and an interest in, the writings and philosophy of Saxon. Police became aware he'd seen Saxon in a TV documentary about Survivalists in the United States.

Gray started writing to Saxon, seeking information about guns and their potential to do harm to other people. 'Gray saw Saxon as a real hope for his expectations,' said police psychologist Miller. 'It's evident from the kind of things Gray was writing to Saxon that he [Gray] was in a disturbed and dangerous state.'

In the letter in which Gray asks for Saxon's advice about the right kind of ammunition to use, Miller believes Gray was seeking approval of, and justification for, his status as a loner, one who lived in paranoia and perceived the need for weapons to defend himself against the outside world.

'Did Saxon give him that approval?' I asked Miller.

'Very much so,' Miller replied. 'And if you want to trace lines of culpability for what ultimately happened in Aramoana, while Saxon wasn't there pulling the trigger, the fact that he offers advice to Gray, and writes stuff that feeds his delusions, means that you could lay some blame right at his doorstep. You simply can't spread this stuff around with impunity, in a world full of disturbed people.'

I asked Saxon whether he had any sense of remorse or understanding concerning the young man in New Zealand who'd been writing to him. Having once been a mental hospital orderly, Gray presumably had some idea about the hair trigger upon which some psychotic minds rest. I put it to him: 'When you read the letters from this young man, surely you must have seen or perceived that here was a guy who was in quite a bad way and needed help?'

'He was just asking for information about guns,' said Saxon with a shrug.

'But here's a young guy in a country many thousands of miles away — a country in which, you'd be aware, we don't need guns to defend ourselves,' I went on.

Saxon appeared in no way concerned at the line of questioning. 'Well, I figured seeing he was a New Zealander he must have been a rational person; I guess he must have been one of those New Zealanders who was crazy. I got it wrong.'

Neil Livingstone, in Washington, shares Miller's conviction that anyone reading between the lines of Gray's correspondence with Saxon would have concluded that this was a young man living right on the edge.

'Here's a guy who was seeking validation and approval,' he told me. 'Through the kind of letters and information that Saxon sent back, he gave Gray that validation and approval. These are the kind of people that mayhem literature appeals to — powerless people, people without influence in society. They don't have productive or meaningful jobs, they don't have power over other people; it's only by acquiring weapons and the ability to terrorise other people that individuals like this gain a sense of power. They really do look to the likes of Kurt Saxon as a kind of spiritual leader, because he affirms them in their desire to get even or gain power through the most horrendous means.'

Saxon seemed singularly unconcerned as I referred him to the passage in *The Poor Man's James Bond* that says an individual who follows his advice has 'the power to destroy many, even hundreds around him.'

'Isn't it entirely possible,' I asked him, 'that Gray read your words and decided, "That's me!" and then acted out a bizarre and murderous fantasy?'

'Well,' said Saxon, 'if he took that from my book he needed more help than I could have given him. As I told you before, from my background I know about mental illness, and if that's the way this young man was, well, perhaps he would have been better off being put to sleep.'

I shook my head and followed up. 'What you're telling me is that if David Gray took your advice, and ended up dead, that wasn't such a bad thing for him and for society?'

'Well and good,' said Saxon quite deliberately.

There's a point during some interviews like this at which your need to contain yourself and go on asking rational questions is overtaken by a kind of outrage that you know everybody who's watching the interview ought to be feeling.

'There were four children among the people Gray murdered that night. Do you have any sense of responsibility towards them?' I asked, almost between gritted teeth.

Without hesitation, Saxon came back, 'No, not at all.' A pause. 'I can't. Does Bush [George Bush Senior, when he was president] feel any responsibility for the misery he's caused in the Middle East?' The question was quite timely — the Gulf War had only just ended — but still Saxon was making no sense.

'George Bush went into Kuwait to throw out an invader,' I pointed out.

'That's as may be,' said Saxon, 'but why weren't the people of Aramoana looking after David Gray?'

By this stage it was obvious there would be no remorse from Kurt Saxon, and that his thinking processes were quite unlike anyone else's I'd ever met. Our talk over the next couple of hours ranged into some almost unbelievable territory — if what we'd heard so far could be called even half believable.

Saxon told us casually — and, I suspect, with a high likelihood of truth — that he had participated in murder, and felt no remorse — rather, some touches of amusement — over what he had done. He told us about the period when he had been a 'Minuteman' — a kind of right-wing militarist — and used to practise using explosives in the Arizona desert, presumably in preparation for the Russian invasion.

He told me how a Minuteman colleague, a young man he'd known quite well, had tried jamming plastic explosive up the exhaust pipe of a car wreck. Saxon described how the man had pushed the explosive charge too hard with a stick, causing an explosion, which had taken off the man's arm. With a macabre grin, Saxon described the man dancing around with blood spurting from the stump where his arm had been, calling for an Army medic.

'Funniest thing I ever saw,' said Saxon with a chuckle. 'That guy had never been in the Army; all that medic business was something he must have gotten off a war movie somewhere.'

I think we were so stunned at that point I forgot to ask how the story ended.

Saxon went on to claim that, along with other Minutemen, he had participated in the murder of a man who had joined their ranks and whom they suspected may have been a communist. He described how, while on 'manoeuvres' in the desert, they had waited till the man's back was turned and then blasted him to death with a shotgun and buried him a long way from the highway.

'Later on we discovered he wasn't a commie after all,' Saxon explained. 'So we got that one wrong — I guess the joke was on us, huh!'

About then, I think all of us in the crew would have been quite content to make a quick exit from the room. We were on the point of making our apologies for not being able to stay for dinner when Saxon's wife started loading up the table with Southern fried chicken, corn bread and a host of other food, which, we almost felt sad to admit, smelled incredibly good. But it was without doubt the most awkward meal I have ever eaten, sitting with a man I knew had such little respect for human life, and trying to make small talk and polite conversation.

A lighter moment — if such a thing was possible in this man's presence — had been the sight, earlier in the evening, of Saxon's two Siamese cats up on the kitchen table, licking the edges of the chocolate chip cheese cake Mrs Saxon had prepared for dessert. I paused the interview at that moment and pointed out to Saxon that Puss and Floss were dealing to the pudding and he might like to intervene.

'Oh, it's OK, don't fret,' said Saxon, without even glancing around. 'They've both been to the vet recently.' End of story — or almost. Director Brett Cammell and I sat across from each other over dessert, exchanging anxious glances, gingerly picking at the cheesecake with our forks, trying desperately to figure out whether we had successfully marshalled the pussies' portions to the edge of our plates. When we felt we'd stayed as long as was polite for dinner with a rural Arkansas maniac, we said goodbye and headed off into the night, anxious to get inside our motel rooms, double bolt the door and have a long shower. Undoubtedly the most mind-blowing day in my journalistic career to date.

Our further inquires established just how frustrated law officials and psychologists like Ian Miller are over the ready availability of mayhem literature around the world. Astonishingly enough, at that time neither Saxon's two volumes of *The Poor Man's James Bond*, nor the equally revolting material of another American author, John Minery, called *How to Kill*, was banned in this country. Although they had been imported by a number of New Zealanders, including David Gray, they had never been submitted for censorship or classification.

In these days of virtually unrestricted access to this kind of material over the Internet, the argument has advanced several stages further, along with the potential for harm. Now a 13-year-old doesn't have to look far to find out how to make a pipe bomb. Who knows what kind of controls concerned agencies might seek to impose on this material in the future? In the meantime, perhaps almost as depressing is the thought that ultimately you can't stop people who are intent on hurting others; people who are motivated by some kind of weird frustration which they feel bound to let loose upon fellow members of society.

The encouragement and counsel people such as Kurt Saxon give the likes of David Gray are undoubtedly very sinister factors, well beyond the control of any legislation. As we wrapped up our report on what had happened at Aramoana in November 1990, we learned Gray had sought the advice of Saxon one last time before his murderous rampage. The irony was that while we were in Harrison interviewing Saxon, the very last book he had sent Gray was making its way back to America from New Zealand, unopened. The scrawled writing on the front of the envelope read: 'Return to sender — recipient deceased'.

As we completed our dealings with Saxon, he showed us one other letter, which seemed to give lie to his claims that his books did no harm. It was from a young man called Tim, in Ohio. Judging by the letter, Tim read Saxon's books religiously — a true devotee. Tim wrote:

> Kurt, could you tell me the best way to administer poison? The main thing is, the death has to be quiet. Also what's the terriblest poison you know of, the kind that causes an agonising death? How do you make it? And how much is a lethal dose? Is there anything you can give to someone who has diabetes, that will make their diabetes bad enough to kill them?

Saxon admitted he knew Tim quite well. 'He's a weird kind of guy and I know he's made a couple of bombs already.'

Despite that knowledge, Saxon said he'd written to Tim and told the young man everything he'd wanted to know.

In his most recent book at the time, before we'd told him about how David Gray and the others at Aramoana had met their end, Kurt Saxon wrote:

> After selling over 50 thousand copies of 'The Poor Man's James Bond', there has not been one report of any youngster hurting himself or anyone else. You can be sure the media would love to smear me with a story of one of my young readers destroying all forms of life in his neighbourhood. Even so, it wouldn't bother me unless I lived in that unfortunate community.

Words which now fairly drip with irony.

Before we left Saxon's home state of Arkansas, we made one other excursion with our camera. About two hours from Harrison, in the Ozark Mountains, there's a monument to the kind of madness Saxon and other mayhem authors have advocated — a deserted Survivalist compound. The local cops had said it would be a useful place to visit to get some perspective on the kind of crazy stuff that had happened in the early 80s in the state. Until you've immersed yourself in such a region, listened to some of the rhetoric on the local talk shows and seen the bumper stickers, you can't imagine how far some people can drift from sanity. You read it on the rear windows of the massive pick-up trucks, right below the triple shotgun rack: 'Sure you can take my gun away from me, when you pry it from my cold dead fingers!' Or, 'Keep honking my friend, I'm just re-loading.'

OK, you figure, some of the good ol' boys do have their tongue firmly planted in their cheek. But the Survivalists are a different breed altogether, feeding off the kind of barely controlled, anti-government fury that drives the Kurt Saxons of the world. Rebelling against tax, and any form of government involvement in life much beyond the printing of postage stamps. There's always a healthy dose of anti-Jewish sentiment thrown in for good measure — deeply held suspicions that all government is underpinned by Zionist conspiracies and brotherhoods.

The compound we visited that day in northern Arkansas had once been occupied by a couple of hundred people — families, with children. But families in which Mum and Dad were firmly of the view that they should take up arms and retreat into the back-woods, inside a fortress. In 1985, the place had been the subject of an FBI raid after the murder of two state troopers in which camp members were suspects. When the Feds moved in on the Sur-vivalists' fort, they found it full of the accoutrements of modern urban terrorism: home-made bombs; containers of deadly poison, cooked up in the compound's own lab; and, lying prominently amongst the debris left by the fleeing Survivalists, a copy of *The Poor Man's James Bond*.

This, then, was a huge part of Saxon's legacy — the incitement of perhaps otherwise normal people to bitterness, paranoia and hatred towards their countrymen. Most of the people who'd lived in the compound had fled before the FBI raid. The ghost-town feeling was unmistakable, as we wandered among piles of cloth-ing, scores of pairs of kids' shoes and sophisticated short-wave radio equipment, and through a sad little schoolhouse. Among the schoolbooks, a child's last lesson — apparently a study on what you do when the government comes and starts shooting everyone. 'Stop, drop and roll,' said the neatly drawn crayon project. We wondered, as we completed our excursion to the South, when and where the next Aramoana might be.

UPDATE

As one might have expected, the Internet has been like manna from heaven for Kurt Saxon. He doesn't need the US postal service to promote his ideas these days — he's there for web surfers to find in a flash. In his 70th year, he is to be found on a site that proclaims: 'The World's Life Support systems are coming apart. It's time you learned to build your own. Our books teach you how to provide for yourself, your loved ones and become an asset to your community.'

3

TRYING TO REMEMBER

There was a phone message waiting for me when I got back from a holiday with my family. It was from the mother of a young woman doctor — a doctor who had suffered a horrendous accident but was fighting hard to rebuild her life, her marriage and her career. Would I be interested in making a documentary about the unfolding story? It would turn out to be a stunning journey.

At 23 years old, Lee Savill had been one of the brightest students in her final year at Auckland Medical School. Marked out for success ever since she'd begun her studies, Lee was a bubbly and energetic young woman with a heart not only for medicine, but also for the poor and destitute. Midway through her medical school training she'd fallen in love with Carl Bouzaid, and the pair had decided they would marry early in 1999.

But before that, Lee wanted to field-test her Spanish, and her nearly complete medical qualifications, in a particularly needy place. She went to work in Honduras, and got caught up in the horrendous cyclone, Hurricane Mitch, which devastated that country at the end of 1998. Lee found herself thrust into the middle of incredible want, but relished the chance to practise her skills in the very midst of a disaster. At one stage during the making of our programme on Lee, I searched TVNZ's archives and found footage of Lee, a forthright young woman being interviewed on her return from Central America, looking and sounding for all the world like a seasoned professional from the international aid scene.

Lee and Carl were married the following January, and, in their wedding video, among the most radiant people on that special day were Lee's proud mum and dad, Kerian and Stuart Savill. Kerian is one of those people whose smile fairly crackles with electricity and who brings a rare energy to everything she does. Stu is a more measured character, but runs the family's thriving business, a leather manufacturing plant, with verve and commitment.

So, it was a momentous time for this family as they farewelled Lee not only into marriage but also into a brand new job — as a house surgeon at Rotorua's main hospital. 'We knew we'd miss her terribly,' says Kerian, 'but that sense of separation was tempered with the knowledge that she'd realised two important dreams in fairly short order.'

Staff at the hospital in Rotorua recognised Lee's enormous potential as they watched this bright and motivated house surgeon quickly reach important learning milestones. It was a busy but very fulfilling time for the young couple. Carl had completed his own university studies and in January 1999 had begun working as a primary school teacher. In May, both Carl and Lee were to be capped at university ceremonies honouring several hard years of work.

But about seven weeks before their graduation, there was to come a day that would change their lives forever. They'd been in Auckland visiting Lee's parents for the weekend. Carl and Lee by this stage had been married just 10 weeks.

They say hindsight gives you 20/20 vision, and Kerian Savill looks back on that weekend with exceptional clarity. 'I can remember the conversation vividly,' she says. 'Lee and I had gone out shopping, and she looked a bit worried. She eventually told me that Carl had pulled out to pass a car on the way up from Rotorua. The cars they were passing had closed up — there was no gap — and they'd only just made it back into the line of traffic. They were nearly wiped out.' Kerian, a woman with a strong Christian faith, says she'd told Lee that morning quite breezily not to worry. 'I said, "I don't think God would allow you to grow up to be so bright, get through med school with flying colours, and then allow you to be wiped out in a road accident."'

But later that evening, as Carl and Lee were driving back to Rotorua, Lee's own worst fears were realised. They were less than an hour from home when Carl badly misread a bend in the road, a couple of kilometres south of Matamata. After overtaking a slower vehicle, Carl found himself unable to avoid an oncoming car, which appeared to have come out of nowhere. The resulting crash at high speed was appalling. It left the driver of the other car bleeding and badly injured. Carl, miraculously, appeared to have escaped major harm. But lying next to him, hanging halfway out of the car door, Lee seemed to be dead.

'She wasn't moving and I feared the worst,' Carl reflects. 'I called out her name, and there was nothing. I got Lee's mum and dad on the cellphone in Auckland as soon as I'd gathered my thoughts and said, "I think she's gone."' Still deeply unconscious, Lee was taken to Waikato Hospital, where she hovered somewhere between life and death in a coma, attached to a bewildering array of life-sustaining equipment.

Everyone who knew Lee held their breath and prayed that the once brilliant young woman would emerge from the coma at least partially normal. Family photographs from this time are incredibly touching. There's a completely comatose Lee, with breathing tubes emerging from her throat and nose, surrounded by brightly coloured balloons, soft toys and a husband and family trying desperately to look hopeful for the camera. There's something about this kind of tragedy that galvanises ordinary New Zealanders: Lee was never alone during those days — there was always someone at her side. But for Carl it was an agonising wait.

'Those days were so tough,' says Carl. 'I knew the only reason Lee was lying there in a coma was because I'd made a stuff-up. I would have given anything for my swerve that night to have been the other way. I wanted to be the one lying there injured, with her looking at *me*.'

Finally, Lee started to wake up. She had that completely vacant stare you so often see in the brain-injured. Her first words as she emerged from her haze were a mixture of the bizarre and comical. Somehow, stuck in her now-jumbled mind were medical terms she had probably wrestled with at exam time. She muttered over and over again about a condition called an 'umbilical hernia'.

In her own way, Lee sounded lucid enough, but it was clear that the 'wiring' in her brain had suffered a major knock in the accident. The other thing that was plain, as she returned to consciousness, was that this man standing beside her bed — who everyone said was her husband — was something of a puzzle to her. She was starting to recall she knew him from somewhere, but as to him being her husband, that memory had apparently completely gone. So had the memories about her career as a doctor. Medical school memories were there, but only vaguely.

The amateur videotape taken by the family as Lee worked her way through the rehabilitation process is almost unbearably sad. Here was a young woman who had graduated near the top of her class in the complex world of medicine struggling with basic word association. 'Are heavy and light opposites?' she is asked. Lee thinks hard and shakes her head.

With her mum, Kerian, in the background and Carl holding the camera, Lee asks plaintively, 'What did I do for a job before I got sick?'

'You were a doctor, in Rotorua,' Kerian tells her patiently.

'Really? I was a doctor?' asks Lee in a voice that sounds more like that of a nine-year-old. Then she starts to cry. 'Am I going to be normal again? It's frustrating that I can't remember, that it's taking so long . . .'

Kerian throws her arms round Lee reassuringly, a relentless cheerleader for her daughter. 'Yes, but you're getting much better. All the time. You've remembered some things today that you hadn't remembered before. That's great. You're doing very well!'

But the sheer reality was this: as in so many cases of traumatic brain injury, it was as if Lee's mind was simultaneously on 'Play' and 'Record'. Not only was her memory of long-past experiences fractured — even, in some cases, completely absent — but new memories could be erased within only hours. This meant Lee and her family could have an enjoyable morning, but by the afternoon all memory of the happy occasion would be gone from Lee's mind.

Lee would look at photos of her wedding. All the marvellous dresses, the flowers, the cake and the entire glittering occasion were now like fresh information to her. That most wonderful of all the days in her life was reduced to nothing but a series of images on photographic paper. Lee had been robbed of the feelings and the experience of that day.

Resumption of anything like a normal life, let alone returning to a challenging career as a doctor, was clearly going to be exceedingly difficult. Lee's colleagues at Rotorua Hospital were being supportive, but the unspoken fear in every heart was that her career as a physician was now well and truly over.

Carl Bouzaid was wracked with a whole range of emotions. As he thought about his driving behaviour that night, and indeed on other occasions when he'd let impatience get the better of him, he started to take in the enormity of what had happened to his new wife. 'Such a hard lesson, such a hard lesson,' he said through his tears as we began a series of interviews with the family, taking the Savills up on their unique offer to allow us to watch Lee's recovery.

Those early interviews with Carl and the Savill family were to produce some very compelling moments of television footage. Carl recounted the shattering experience he and Lee had had when they'd first tried to put their marriage back together, at a rehabilitation home in suburban Auckland.

The Rehab Plus centre provides small apartments on site where people can try to lead something approaching a normal life while continuing to rebuild the life of the injured person. It had been decided that the concept of trying to be a married woman again would be too much for Lee, given the enormous gaps in her memory concerning Carl. So, on Lee and Carl's first night in the rehab flat, Stu and Kerian came for dinner. There were more poignant videotaped moments as Lee once again asked about events that had taken place only hours before but which she could not now remember. There had been multiple visits to her parents' home since the crash, but all recollection of these had also gone.

'I feel so stupid,' Lee said to Kerian as they did the dishes in the kitchen that evening. 'I can't even remember marrying Carl.'

Kerian, as she always did, tried to be totally reassuring and affirming. 'That's OK,' she told Lee, 'one day you'll wake up and it'll all come back, and you'll be able to say "I remember marrying you!"'

But when Stu and Kerian departed that evening, leaving Carl and Lee to themselves, the outcome was not happy. 'At three o'clock in the morning she woke up,' says Carl. 'She was very distressed — she couldn't remember anything that had happened even an hour or two before; it was like she was blacking out and waking up new and had a whole heap of questions. She was asking "Where am I?" and "What am I doing here?"'

With hindsight, Kerian said they should have foreseen this. 'We feel thick about it now,' she said wistfully. 'We didn't realise that for her to wake up with Carl beside her was just crazy. She was back at about eighteen or sixteen in her memory, and here was this man beside her. It didn't make sense to Lee.'

Lee would drop back off to sleep, then wake again an hour later with the same questions, the same confusion. 'We called Lee's mum and dad at about three in the morning,' says Carl. 'They talked to her for a while and settled her down, but then the same thing all over again: she'd wake up, blank. "Where am I? Who's this?" And then, "Mum and Dad. I want Mum and Dad."'

It was an incredibly sad and disappointing outcome. The rehab arrangement obviously wasn't going to work. So, after a lot of soul-searching by the whole family, Lee moved home to be with her parents again, leaving Carl on his own. In one sense it felt like a huge step backwards, given everyone's high expectations. The family waited and prayed for the marriage to regain some meaning for the still confused young woman.

Carl, now wrestling seriously with guilt and anguish over the crash, had to face up to the fact that he'd need to win his wife's heart all over again. So he'd visit the Savill home, effectively as boyfriend, in a bid to court Lee afresh. The shaky am-cam footage from those days is extremely moving. There's Carl, the eager suitor, bringing Lee flowers, eliciting from the young woman just a flicker of what once had been.

'That's really cool,' she says in her still rather flat tone. 'I love you.'

By late May, Lee seemed to be well on the road to accepting Carl as her husband. But every now and then there'd be a bad day. She would suddenly decide this man they all said was her spouse was not who she wanted to be with.

'I arrived here early one Sunday morning,' Carl remembers. 'It was great to see everyone and say hello and then get ready to go to church, but it turned out Lee had said to Kerian, "What's *he* doing here? I don't want to go to church with him."' On days like this Carl felt terrible and wondered whether things would ever get back to normal.

In the midst of all the uncertainty there came a day of reckoning for Carl with the justice system. The crash that had caused Lee's injuries was undoubtedly his fault. Some fairly hefty charges had to be faced. Family and friends prayed with him outside the court, then supported him inside as he faced the judge. Carl sat in the front row at the Auckland District Court, flanked by his wife and his in-laws. In Stu Savill's hand, a letter he'd written to the judge expressing the family's unconditional support for Carl and asking for leniency. On Kerian's lap, a copy of a book by Philip Yancey, entitled *What's So Amazing About Grace?*

The judge sentenced Carl to 12 months' disqualification from driving. There would be some exceptions, to enable Carl to take Lee to places she needed to go to to continue her recovery.

In journalism you spend a lot of time listening to people lay blame and demand recompense. For me, as a reporter, it was hard not to wonder whether Stu and Kerian ever felt angry at Carl over what had happened to Lee — but in all of our interviews there was never a flicker of animosity.

'Carl made a mistake, and I think I made a conscious decision to say, OK, this could've happened to anyone.' Kerian eyeballs you firmly as she spells out her views on her son-in-law. 'It must be extremely hard for Carl. I decided I've got to keep a good attitude, stay positive and get on. I actually remember being angry about it and upset, but my forgiveness is complete.'

Stu was equally straightforward. 'He's our son — they're one flesh now. You hurt Carl, you're going to hurt Lee as well.'

It was at about this point in the story that I started to get to know Lee quite well. She has one of those extremely open and trusting faces that gives an impression of overdeveloped innocence. At that stage of her life the effect was especially pronounced. As I sat with her filming our first interview one afternoon, she spoke in a strikingly unaffected way about her dreams and about getting to know and love Carl all over again.

Only a week or so before our first meeting, there had been

quite a breakthrough. They'd all decided Lee had made enough progress for Carl to move into Stu and Kerian's home to stay, like a guest, in the spare bedroom. It was a small step towards seeing whether Lee could handle having him around a bit more.

Within a couple of weeks, a big change. Carl told me quite excitedly: 'She walked into the bedroom the other night and said, "I think I should be in here with you — we're married." She'd obviously been processing it and realising that "OK, Carl's my husband, why am I in a different room?" And for whatever reason, it came to pass that we started sharing a bed again.'

I said to Lee during our first filmed interview, 'That must have been quite an evening.'

'Well I don't remember it, but I guess it was, especially for him.'

So here she was: a young woman aware that she really was married, but with a mind still so affected, 12 weeks after the crash, that day-to-day memories were even now fading away like vapours.

Even so, during that first encounter with me, Lee indicated she was starting to wake up to the reality that she was married. Furthermore, while working at her mum and dad's leather factory, where it was plain to see she had great manual dexterity, she was remembering that she'd trained as a doctor. But getting well enough even to consider going back into a ward and being a house surgeon again was obviously a huge hurdle. Nonetheless, Lee, in her own way, was full of childlike optimism.

'Do you think you're going to practise medicine again?' I asked.

'Definitely,' she replied.

'What makes you confident?' I asked.

'I think it's my dreams,' said Lee, and then her face broke into a beautiful smile. 'I've had all sorts of funny dreams that always involve medicine and I can't imagine doing anything else. I believe I'm constantly improving, so eventually I'll get to the point where I'll be able to practise again.'

She was trying very hard. Down in her study, well-thumbed medical textbooks lay around, and Lee would spend long hours leafing through the heavy tomes, seeking to make the vital connections all over again.

But what lay before Lee was a barrage of tests and assessments ordered by the Medical Council of New Zealand. The council had quite clear procedures for doctors, like Lee, who'd suffered a brain injury. Before she could be considered fit to resume either training or medical practice, she would need to persuade the authorities she was functioning again at full capacity — for her own, and patients', protection. Although her memory was, to her own way of thinking, starting to improve, the road ahead was going to be extremely tough.

As Lee grew physically stronger she took the initiative of enlisting the help of a friend, a house surgeon at Auckland Hospital called Dr Andrew Cameron. Andrew and one of the senior consultants at the hospital both knew that before her accident Lee had had huge potential, and they hoped it would only be a matter of time before she was well enough to be a house surgeon again. Whenever he could manage it, Andrew would arrange for Lee to come on ward rounds with him, so she could get the feel of being among patients and medical colleagues all over again.

It was a huge confidence builder for Lee. Carl would take her to the hospital in the morning and, with the little video camera we'd given them, conduct touching interviews with her as she tentatively put her stethoscope round her neck and prepared to head into the high-pressured medical environment.

'Why did you want to come back?' Carl asks one morning as Lee looks nervously up at the ward sign. Lee replies, a little hesitantly: 'Because if my goal is to be a doctor again, the only way I can do that is by coming here.'

'OK, what are you going to do today?' asks Carl.

'Ward rounds,' says Lee. 'Looking at patients.'

'What will you do?'

'Observe, just observe.'

'Well, I hope you have a wonderful morning,' says Carl with his characteristic enthusiasm. 'I love you.'

'I love you too,' Lee replies, and then moves with as much confidence as she can muster into the ward.

Lee's excursions among multiple patients and through thick medical files and drug records went well. All she was allowed to do for now was take notes and listen, but she'd emerge proudly after a few hours with an exercise book full of the patient details she'd written down, and run through the notes for Carl with barely suppressed excitement.

Lee's passion for medicine was still very much there, but she continued to experience huge bouts of frustration because of her inability to recall large chunks of her training, and also the continuing plague of short-term memory deficit. By taking copious notes she hoped she'd ultimately be able to persuade the authorities, and of course herself, that she had the power of retention.

The trouble was, Lee needed detailed reminders just to attend to basic tasks. One day when we were filming at the Savill home, Lee showed me her bathroom list — a small whiteboard with a series of boxes and ticks to keep her in the flow of a daily routine. A tick needed to go in a box when she'd completed a basic task like washing her hair, cleaning her teeth or taking a couple of small items of medication.

It was a little bewildering, and quite tragic in its own way. I was wondering how a young woman, who still needed reminders like this, was ever going to make it back into medicine, but Lee and all her family continued to express huge measures of confidence. They were all on such a complex journey of discovery into this phenomenon called brain injury. It was sad yet fascinating to watch Lee play the piano, for example. In her scrambled mind that particular skill had been retained intact, but as she played the same piece twice in a row, she'd perform it brilliantly one moment, then badly the next.

There was another complication that was not proving easy to resolve. The return to a normal married life for Carl and Lee was far from straightforward. Intimacy was difficult. The couple were now sleeping in the same bed at Stu and Kerian's home, but for the time being there was no sex. There was a sad, yet humorous interview at this point.

'The sex thing must be quite demanding for you both,' I offered gingerly.

There was no trace of hesitation from Lee. 'Probably more so for Carl. I'm asleep so I don't know.'

'What do you think it's going to take to get back to normal?'

Lee shook her head. 'Who knows? The thing is at the moment with having such a poor memory we'll have sex and I won't remember it in the morning. So not much point.'

Right through this time, Carl, not having resumed his teaching career so as to be able to spend more time with Lee, took on the role of her cheerleader and trainer. They ran together as often as they could to keep up Lee's physical strength.

One afternoon as they finished a training run up on Mt Eden, we were there filming, and they announced there'd been what seemed like a breakthrough. Together Carl and Lee had come to a decision to try having their honeymoon at an Auckland hotel all over again.

'Whose idea was that?' I asked.

Lee shook her head. 'Can't remember,' she said.

'I think it was both of us,' said Carl enthusiastically. 'We're looking forward to Thursday night.'

Lee nodded with some hesitancy. 'I think it's going to be good,' she said.

But the attempt to begin married life all over again at the honeymoon hotel had a more modest outcome than Carl had been anticipating, as it transpired Lee wanted something more like a holiday than a honeymoon. There was some progress in their lovemaking, but it was tentative.

Carl realised there was still a long way to go and he'd need to make some major personal adjustments. It was a powerful and tearful moment for him as we interviewed him the following week.

'You love her a lot, don't you?' I asked.

'Yeah, I do,' said Carl. 'I just want her to go on, get better, and I don't want to do anything that's going to stop that. It's as simple as that, so sex isn't going to help her if I'm demanding it, you know, and in true love you don't demand things of people.'

As we were filming at this point, we were reminded of some of the grim statistics we'd heard along the way — the reality that many marriages didn't survive such testing times. Brain injury is a rock on which many relationships that encounter it founder, because the demands it makes of people is more than many can take. But Carl and Lee, despite the rocky road, seemed determined to get it right.

On an overcast morning, six months to the day after the awful road crash, Carl, Lee, Stu and Kerian stood on the top of Mt Eden, just above the Savills' home, watching the sun come up. They all had a strong personal faith, which had helped them through the previous few months of trial and tears, and that morning they went to the hilltop to offer a brief prayer of thanks and to express a strong sense of hope for the future. Lee's mates from medical school had spelled out her name in big rocks down in the crater.

This was a special day for Lee in another way, because she was going to graduate as a doctor from Auckland Medical School. She had been too sick to attend the capping ceremony in May, but now, on a supplementary capping day in mid-September, she would march with hundreds of others up Queen Street to be officially declared a doctor in the Auckland Town Hall.

Back at the house, a fabulous morning barbecue with champagne was waiting. But the day had something of a hollow ring for the family. As they came down the mountain for the celebration breakfast, they dwelt glumly on the fact that, for the time being at least, Lee's degree was of no practical use: she had no job in a hospital and wasn't even allowed to fill a syringe. Midway through breakfast Lee was a little morose and let her frustration out.

'A light at the end of the tunnel? I'm not sure. I just think is there any end to it, you know? I get ticked off wondering am I ever going to get to the point where I can remember enough to function.'

'We're actually glad she's at this point,' said her dad, reaching across the table to hold her hand. 'We've been told that an important part of the grieving process is not simply anger, but the ability to confront and express your frustration. We've almost been anticipating this happening with Lee. I guess it's hard for all of us, but at least she's not bottling it up.'

It was hard for the crew and I not to develop a lump in the throat as we watched Lee trying on her gown and cap and pondering the implications of being awarded a degree that for now she couldn't use.

Still, later in the day Lee was glad she'd made the effort to be capped. She marched purposefully up Queen Street with the others. The loudest cheers in the town hall that afternoon came from Carl, Stu and Kerian as Lee walked proudly to the podium and was officially declared to be Dr Lee Savill, Bachelor of Medicine, Bachelor of Surgery.

In the weeks that followed, Lee began in earnest her fight to be recognised as competent enough to resume medical training. Dr Kris Fernando, Lee's neuropsychologist, put her through a stringent series of tests. Tests of word association, number recognition, memory and verbal comprehension. Tests which got tougher with each session. Sitting in on the exam, we saw the limits of Lee's ability become painfully obvious.

Fernando is a compassionate but straightforward woman. As I interviewed her later for our documentary, she held up a model of the human brain and stressed how much damage can be caused when the fragile organ gets slammed around inside the skull by the massive forces of deceleration associated with a motor vehicle crash at high speed. She left everyone in no doubt that Lee would have to do much better in her next test if she was to get enough ticks in enough boxes in the ultimate report to the medical council.

Lee kept reading her medical textbooks. She applied with ruthless determination to Lakeland Health in Rotorua, her old employer, for the opportunity to go back into the wards — as an observer. She wasn't pushing for the right to resume her training at this time, just to be able to do what she'd done on several occasions in Auckland — to watch, and to familiarise herself with the environment in which she so passionately wanted to work again.

'I want to go in, sort of like a student,' Lee reflected one day during an interview with me. 'I think the patients would have a right to be worried if they knew they were with a doctor who'd had a head injury.'

'What is it you love about medicine so much?' I wanted to know.

Lee thought for a moment. It was as if I could see her going back in her mind to Honduras, where she'd worked so hard in those last few months as a medical student before the crash.

'Just helping other people, I think, is the biggest thing. And it's not only doing something physical, it's actually using your mind. But more than that, it's helping people who aren't so fortunate.'

About nine months after the crash, milestones were coming quickly for Lee Savill. Having passed her eyesight tests, she was allowed to drive a car again and found she was able to sit at her old piano and play a complete piece of music, twice over, with no mistakes. What's more, she and Carl had made a big decision. They'd move back to Rotorua so Carl could resume his teaching career and Lee could await final word from Lakeland Health about being allowed back into the hospital wards as an observer.

Writing and applying from Auckland, the young couple found dealing with the health board a painfully slow process. Thinking they'd just about cleared all the hurdles, they'd encounter another welter of red tape.

'I kind of feel like they're afraid to let me do anything at all,' Lee said ruefully one day. She was diligently working her way through all her old medical textbooks, studying long into the night — everything from basic items of anatomy to the advanced principles of human cell biology. She was pleased with how much she was remembering. But being allowed back into the wards was going to be complex. When pressed on the subject, both Carl and Lee had to admit they knew the hospital did have to cover all the bases legally — even if it let Lee back in a limited capacity.

We were with the Savills the day Carl and Lee finally packed up the car and set out for Rotorua to try to restart their life. 'You look after her!' Kerian whispered urgently into Carl's ear in the driveway. 'And look after yourself!' she added hurriedly, giving him one of her characteristic bear hugs. After the goodbyes in Auckland, I joined Lee and Carl on the drive south.

About two hours later, I drove with Carl and Lee past the spot where, nine months earlier, everything had broken apart in their lives. We stood at the corner to record a few moments of interview. Watching Lee, I wondered whether this would be a tough and emotionally wrenching experience. Looking hard at the bend in the road, Carl shook his head and said in a voice just above a whisper: 'I can't believe I did it. Seeing it in daylight it's so clear what a crazy manoeuvre it was.'

Lee looked vacantly down the road. 'I have no bad feelings towards this place,' she said. 'I have no memory of that night, which I guess in its own way is not such a bad thing.'

After a few moments of contemplation they climbed back into the car and continued to Rotorua, arriving later that day to set up in a small flat in the grounds of the hospital. Now they would have to play a waiting game as, over the following weeks, committees, officials and supervisors met and talked to determine whether Lee would be given the chance to make a fresh start.

There were encouraging times as they waited — including when they met a young doctor a little bit older than Lee who had suffered a major head injury after falling off a mountain bike a couple of years earlier. He had overcome huge odds to return to practice. It was another good confidence builder for Lee; proof that you could suffer brain injury and make it all the way back to performing competently in a demanding job.

While documenting Lee's journey, we had an end point in mind for our story. I wanted to be there with a camera on the day Lee finally put on her white coat, stethoscope and ID badge and walked into the ward at Rotorua Hospital to begin observing. But as time passed, it seemed there were so many barriers to this happening we might never get that magic piece of footage.

Lee confided in Kerian that she felt dreadfully frustrated and disheartened at times. 'We would have these quite heartbreaking conversations,' says Kerian. 'In one sense I had a bright, lovely adult daughter on the other end of the phone, but often it felt like I was helping to console a grief-stricken child.'

But right through this period, the bad days were often offset by times of delight. One day as we were filming, one of those unexpected breakthroughs came for Lee. She and Carl had been looking back through some of the photos of their wedding and honeymoon, and Lee suddenly began describing in great detail the room in which they'd spent one of their first days together as a married couple. It was a memory that had apparently been completely lost but now had been recaptured. Lee was able to tell Carl a whole list of things she recalled about the motel in the Bay of Islands.

'It's so exciting,' Carl enthused as we interviewed them. 'This morning before you got here, as we woke up, Lee remembered a whole bunch of stuff about a woman patient she had helped when she was a new doctor at Rotorua. That must've been a couple of weeks before the crash, and that's such a huge step forward. There've been two things we've been hoping and praying for — "married memories" and "doctor memories" — and now she's getting both. The strides are enormous.'

That morning I saw a light go on in Lee's eyes I hadn't seen before. The implications of better recall were having a joyful impact on her morale.

That morning we also recorded perhaps the most touching interview of all. Lee and Carl opened up on how they felt about each other. They were quite honest about the fact that there had been some enormously testing and difficult times over the previous nine months, but each was now swearing allegiance to the other in their marriage, asserting that the terrible things they'd had to endure had not only brought them closer together, but had also made them understand that real love was about more than simply feelings and appearance: it had to do with commitment, a decision to love despite life's misfortunes.

There were no gilt edges to this relationship: it could clearly often be as raw and demanding as any marriage, but these people had something quite powerful going for them in the midst of their trial.

Lee and Carl had tremendous friends working on their behalf within Rotorua Hospital; people trying hard behind the scenes to see whether they could advance the process of at least getting Lee into the hospital system and starting to learn again.

In early 2000 Carl gleefully delivered to me two pieces of videotape he'd recorded at their flat. One was a scene shot on Christmas Day, showing Lee opening her present, a handbag. Carl is laughing hilariously in the background as he films. The reason? Lee actually asked for the bag before Christmas, and then, with her still faltering memory, completely forgot— making it so much easier for Carl to surprise her.

'Isn't it great having a wife who can still forget things? Surprises are a cinch!'

Fast forward to 5 May. This videotape is grainy but even more poignant. Carl is taking the phone through to Lee in bed late one Sunday evening.

'What is it, what is it?' says Lee, as she wakes up out of her haze. Carl hands Lee the phone, and a smile of sheer unaffected delight spreads across the young woman's face. The news is that she's to be allowed back into the hospital to resume her training. Her dream of working towards being a competent, fully-fledged doctor has finally been given wings once more.

We were indeed there with a camera, with Lee, on the day she finally put on her white coat, stethoscope and hospital ID badge and walked proudly up the hill with Carl and her parents to start work. We all got a bit misty-eyed that morning. Dr Savill was back — not yet able to practise her craft as a fully qualified physician, but out of the starting blocks.

'We've all learned so much in the last year,' said Stu, as we walked up the path to the hospital. 'I would never have believed how much was involved in the rebuilding of a human existence. We saw Lee's life stripped away to nothing, then put back together, and we're very grateful.'

The story, of course, had yet to reach a fairy-tale ending. It was going to take Lee a long time still to regain all those things she'd lost, and to persuade her neuropsychologist she was capable of making it as a physician. A year-and-a-half after walking back onto the wards at Rotorua Hospital, she was still working towards this ultimate goal.

But Lee was not disheartened. Recently she completed a gruelling course at Outward Bound, and sent an email to all her friends, marking her accomplishment and talking about the future:

> For the past 18 months I have been working as an observer at Rotorua Hospital. Over time I have done more and more work. I'm not employed by the hospital yet and so don't get paid for the work I do. At Outward Bound, I developed in my confidence, and taking initiative. These are the two areas that I have struggled in since the accident.
>
> I can now admit a patient and no longer look for recognition of my efforts. I am confident enough to know in myself that I have done a good job. I am also working on taking more initiative. I now try not to ask Carl whether I should do something or not. I just do it, within reason.
>
> My hope is that next year I will begin working again as a paid doctor. However, it would need to be in a job-share situation. I do not handle the long hours required of doctors. So perhaps I could job share with a mother, or someone studying for exams etc.
>
> I'd like to thank everyone who has been praying for me over the past two and a half years. I know there are many of you still faithfully praying. Don't stop now though. Please

pray for a part time or job share position for me for next year.

Thank you very much.
Love from Lee.

UPDATE

As I completed this chapter, Lee undertook a crucial test: the neuropsychological analysis to determine whether she'd be fit to resume practice as a doctor. She was nervous but determined as she came to Auckland for the half-day session with Dr Kris Fernando. Among the questions Lee was asked in the test: Had she given any thought to what she might do for a career if she was not found fit to be a physician? Lee said there was nothing else she wanted to do.

A couple of weeks later, the results of the test were back. The news was not good. Lee's memory had not improved to the point that Fernando could recommend — for now at least — that she be allowed registration. There were tears and sadness on the day she went back into the hospital and handed in her pager. 'I feel like the mother of a child that's just died,' she told me over the phone. Within days of receiving the medical report, Lee was starting to consider other possibilities — maybe a position on the staff at her church. Has the dream of being a doctor died altogether? It's probably too early to tell.

Those who love Lee the most simply hope and pray her dreams come true.

4

ALIEN ENCOUNTERS

Back in the early 1990s a little-known American TV writer suddenly found himself the focus of international attention. Chris Carter had stumbled on a concept for a hit series, which had started to assume cult status, not only in the United States but also around the world. It wasn't only the presence in his show of the flame-haired beauty Gillian Anderson that accounted for its popularity (although by the end of the century websites featuring Anderson would be the most visited on the entire Internet); nor was it the smouldering charm of David Duchovny, former host of a late-night TV soft-porn show. It was more that Carter had devised a TV programme that skirted the edge of something quite fascinating: the almost respectable belief that we are not alone in the universe.

Nicely branded with the memorable tag line 'The truth is out there', *The X-Files* unashamedly drew plot lines from everywhere, including the various permutations of the Roswell Affair, hokey tales about female 'Bigfoots' and radiation-contaminated Russians who could slip in and out of sewer drains and suck your brains.

What fascinated me about the *X-Files* era was that, in the mid-1990s, the TV series and its spin-offs were going hand in hand with some startling research into aliens conducted by people with the academic status of eminent Harvard psychiatrists and the like. The writings of one particular authority in this field caught my eye in the newspaper one Saturday morning.

Dr John Mack — a Harvard don — had recently interviewed a range of people who were sure they had been abducted by aliens and had had a variety of eye-popping cosmic experiences. The interesting part was that Dr Mack, to the serious consternation of many of his colleagues, was giving a huge amount of credence to the stories, and had written them up in what purported to be a weighty analytical work, called *Abductions*.

As a journalist, you find after a few years you have a mind made up of a variety of mental Manila files, into which are thrust those ideas you sometimes think would make a great story — if only you could find the excuse to turn them into a cogent piece of writing. In my mind that morning I shuffled together the newspaper clipping about John Mack and my musings from a couple of years earlier about an ad I had seen for an unusual 'support group'. That ad had invited to a meeting any New Zealanders who wanted to share their experiences of being abducted by aliens. Dead serious.

Whatever happened at that meeting, I wondered? After a bit of digging in the office the following Monday, I came up with the startling discovery that in excess of 500 people had turned up at the Auckland get-together to talk about encounters with aliens. A TV crew had also been present, and when I'd traced the footage, there they all were — packing a high-school auditorium and talking with great earnestness about having been taken up into spaceships and subjected to weird experiments, and having 'lost time' on various occasions.

This was to lead me on one of the most fascinating journalistic detours I've ever been on, allowing me to meet, and try to delve into the minds of, those who swear blind they've been places that would boggle the mind of even a Fox Mulder or Dana Scully.

We — a camera crew, director Brett Cammell and I — first met them in a draughty, out-of-the-way community centre on a Tuesday night in South Auckland. They sat in a rough circle on rickety old chairs. 'We're abductees,' they told us, without a trace of a smirk and with great seriousness. 'That's what we all have in common,' said a young man, who turned out to be the produce manager of a local supermarket.

'We draw strength from meeting with others who don't laugh

Diana Routley — off on another adventure.

Alan Routley with Diana – off to a Mozart concert.

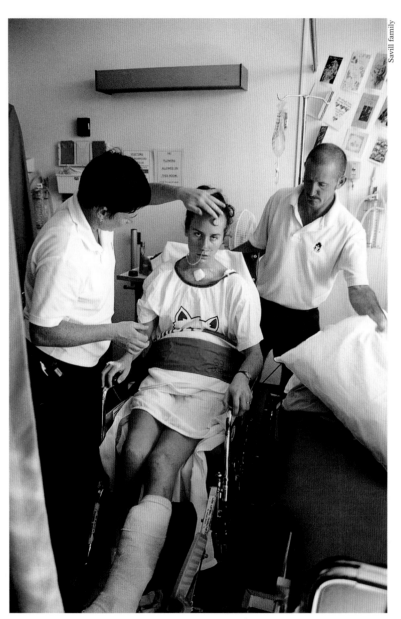

Lee Savill slowly wakes out of her coma, April 1999.

Lee Savill is capped Bachelor of Medicine, Bachelor of Surgery,
Auckland Town Hall, September 1999.

Andrew, Kate and Josh Dominikovich.

David Green

David Green with physiotherapist Suzie Mudge.

Judy Moore at Berane Refugee Camp.

Rob Harley tapes Judy Moore at a World Vision agricultural project in Montenegro.

For 34 hours in November 1990, David Gray held the tiny village of Aramoana in a state of siege.

The house where David Gray fired his final shots. Bullet holes can be seen in the glass door.

A Port Chalmers firefighter dampens hotspots in the ruins of David Gray's torched crib at Aramoana. Only the chimney and fridge survived the flames.

at us or deride us,' said another, a well-coiffured middle-aged woman, smartly dressed, with a tale to tell that evening about how she'd suffered severe pain only the other night from an 'implant' aliens had placed inside her.

Another woman, called Iris, a mother of three with a very responsible job in the health service in South Auckland, described how a probe had been inserted into her head during her last alien encounter.

'Kind of like a beam of white light,' she told everybody. 'As it went into my head it had something like finger things on it, which sort of spread out inside.' The others sat nodding with recognition and understanding.

'There was no fear attached and no pain experienced at the time, which is quite good, I suppose,' said Iris with a slight smile, 'but it's still tender on the top of my head.' And she rubbed the spot where she firmly believed the alien probe had been inserted only a couple of nights earlier.

The dozen or so members of the abduction support group listened to each other intently, sometimes making expressions of real concern as a member struggled to relate something that evidently had a degree of pain attached to it.

Donene, from West Auckland, got a bit emotional as she spoke. 'I thought to myself, "Oh no, they're here again!" But it was more like a shaking, kind of vibrating inside me.' More nodding by now, as Donene went on to articulate something many of the group evidently felt they had experienced at the hands of aliens. 'Terrible, terrible pain in my back passage.'

Collective wince, especially from the camera crew. Donene went on: 'And I got out of bed, and literally staggered and crawled to the toilet, and sat there, and I thought I was being quite quiet, but the pain was so bad I was sobbing.'

Sitting next to Donene, a young man called Robert looked on sympathetically. Relating his latest encounter with extraterrestrials he said, 'There was one I'd never seen before. It looked like a "small grey". It had a kind of crest on its head, a central crest and two sort of crests down the side, so I was wondering if anybody else had seen anything like that?'

'Small greys' featured regularly in the group's conversation.

'A small grey?' I asked innocently. They looked at me as if I was a mildly retarded child — kindly and with patience. 'That's because they're small and they're grey,' said Syd, the produce manager. A small ripple of laughter round the room — half-sympathetic, half-knowing, I thought.

Syd was a genial young man, full of information about his numerous abduction experiences. 'The aliens that most people see when they're relating abduction experiences are small greys.'

Iris went on to explain carefully. Small greys were known to virtually all the attenders: nocturnal visitors whose appearance typically preceded an abductee's being taken from his or her bed and transported by who knows what means to an alien spaceship, where unspeakable things took place.

'They're usually between three and four feet tall.'

'There are taller ones,' Syd chimed in.

'There's such a range of contact going on,' said Julia, over in the corner. Well spoken, with a slight English accent, Julia said her own contact experience included seeing 'blue light beings', beings without a physical form and others only a few centimetres tall. 'I've seen some about the height of tall trees — I saw those in Helensville.'

This was heady stuff. A bunch of people totally in sync with each other and ready to believe just about anything. People quite unmoved by the hilarity their stories predictably arouse; by the jokes about little green men, and tabloid headlines like 'Aliens Stole My Baby'. Point out that there isn't a skerrick of evidence to support any of their stories, and you only make them more determined and focused.

'I didn't want this in my life,' Iris said, adamantly. 'I wanted it not to be there, to go away. A lot of what these so-called experts and debunkers don't realise is that for most of us, initially, we wished it wasn't happening to us. It's not nice.' We left the little hall that night having secured promises from members of the group to come to the studio the following week to share their stories with us in more detail.

Over a long career in journalism, it's fair to say you go away from many of the stories you are forced to go out at night to cover feeling pretty diffident. But this was different: the crew was about as animated in its discussion as any I've seen after a shoot. You sense, as a storyteller, that no matter how you handle this kind of material you almost can't lose. It's all just so downright fascinating.

We faced the challenge, however, of trying to make an intelligent documentary that didn't look as if it was setting out to pass judgement on people like those in the support group, but was trying, at least, to bring some context to what was, after all, a pretty amazing series of claims.

So what was the overall deal here? Peeling back the layers, you realise there's something about space, and what's 'out there', that fills us with a mixture of wonder, fear and occasionally surprise. Hollywood and a couple of million book writers know the value of plumbing our fears, uncertainties and dreams.

Whether it's the kind of alien that kept Sigourney Weaver busy for a seemingly never-ending series, or the extensive variety of ETs investigated by Mulder and Scully, this is fertile ground. No wonder, for example, that the generation raised on these kinds of stories turned on in droves when the alleged autopsy of a supposed alien purportedly recovered near Roswell, New Mexico, was screened on television in mid-1995.

A TVNZ poll after the programme had been aired found 76 per cent of respondents ready to believe the autopsy and alien were real, with only 24 per cent being nay-sayers.

To the sceptics, of course, the emergence of ET believers like Harvard Professor John Mack as high priests of the movement is only a sign that no matter how well educated a person may be, he or she can still be inherently gullible. Furthermore, the fact that four million Americans in a poll in the mid-1990s claimed to have had abduction experiences, including seeing lights, 'losing time' or waking up in the morning with unexplainable marks on their body, simply prompts sceptics to say, 'There's more than one born every minute.'

The business of marks on bodies was a topic of enthusiastic conversation when we had further meetings with the abductees. Get Iris going on the bruises that she says are a regular part of her night-time encounters with small greys, for example. The arm she proffered our cameraman did indeed have some bruises halfway up, and Iris steadfastly insisted they had appeared in the morning, after a night during which she had been transported to an alien operating theatre.

'How did they get there?' Iris asked us pointedly. 'I sleep in my bed alone — it's not like there's anybody else in there grabbing me and making marks on me — so what do you reckon?' By now, of course, we were starting to ask, 'Are these guys for real? Are they putting us on? Are we being led to the point where somebody is going to stand up and loudly proclaim "April fool, April fool"?'

In the weeks that followed, we were to discover the answer was absolutely not. As we began to research accounts from around the world, some very consistent threads began to emerge, such as the shape and size of aliens seen by abductees, and the kinds of experiments done on humans by these beastly creatures.

What the abductees appeared to have in common, in New Zealand and all round the world, was a kind of helplessness as they found themselves, usually in the middle of the night, on cold slabs or benches, often naked, having various bits of their body probed by small greys or other aliens. Aliens intent on either placing tracking devices in their bodies, or, in the case of a number of women abductees, impregnating them with various hideous purposes in mind, including the creation of hybrid babies — half-human, half-alien.

Also very common are tales of paralysis, a bit like the stories you hear from people who haven't been adequately anaesthetised before surgery and can feel the pain of the operation but are unable to cry out for help or resist what's being done. Such stories have become legion in the last few years, and have provided great fodder for movie-makers.

Trying to get to know a little more about the New Zealand abductees, we spent time with some of them during their daily routines. To look at Iris — the woman with the bruises — you'd probably conclude, without knowing anything about her, that she was an extremely normal person. Her job in the health service was complex and responsible, and there was no indication that she was anything other than competent.

The thing that makes Iris different is her adamant assertion that for most of her life, ever since she was six years old, she's been having night-time experiences involving aliens. Among the most traumatic, she said, was the removal of a foetus when she was several weeks pregnant. 'There were beings around the table,' she said during an extensive follow-up interview with us in the studio. 'They inserted something like a cylinder in my vagina and it was extremely painful, and when it was over they showed me the cylinder and there was a foetus inside. They told me the baby was mine, but it was also theirs.' What's more, says Iris, after that experience she was no longer pregnant.

'Where they take you, and I'm assuming it's a space ship, they have this place called the nursery. They take you there and there are a lot of babies of different ages. You're never there alone; there are always other human people there, and they get you to pick the babies up and hold them.'

Other abductees we interviewed had similar tales. The collective wisdom seemed to be that the reason the current crop of aliens is doing such intrusive stuff is that their own race, from the far side of the galaxy, is dying out, and they need bodies like Iris's to help regenerate it.

Iris, left to her own experiences, might well conclude she is completely and utterly insane. But what has strengthened her resolve are her new-found friends in the abduction support group. She's discovered people who've become real soul mates — people like Syd, the supermarket produce manager. He reckons he's had experiences very like Iris's, encounters he related to us with remarkable candour and certainty during his extended interview with our programme.

'There's two ways they get you,' Syd explained. 'You either physically leave the planet or they come to you.'

'Can they walk through walls?' I asked him.

'Oh yeah,' said Syd quickly, 'they've done that several times.'

Syd, like Iris, was a thoroughly regular person — holding down a good job and in a stable relationship. Maybe he had an over-developed interest in building models from the TV series *Star Trek*, but it struck us there were as many nonabductees as abductees who have a fascination for that kind of thing. What makes Syd a little different is that he believes extraterrestrials have taken his semen and used it to make hybrid alien beings.

'They're still taking semen samples and still using the anal probes — I'm not sure why. The semen samples are used for cross-production, reproduction. I haven't been able to figure out the anal probes,' he said with a bemused shake of the head. 'Don't know that I ever will.'

Being hard-bitten, cynical journalists, we regularly had it on the tip of our tongue during these interviews to ask why highly developed life forms would travel light years across the universe to spend their time sticking things up the bottoms of supermarket produce managers, but a sense of decorum and an awareness of the need to be even-handed stopped us from being so crass.

Seriously, though — when it comes to all these stories of probes and impregnations, it's been suggested on more than a few occasions in recent years, by psychologists and psychoanalysts, that their frequency and abundance are part of the phenomenon of adults trying to rationalise severe childhood trauma.

We raised this possibility with Donene — the woman who spoke fearfully about her 'back passage' problems after a recent alien encounter. 'I've heard that kind of suggestion put forward,' she said, 'and I'd have to concede that I was sexually abused as a young person. But these experiences I'm relating are different — very different.'

By this stage, as you can imagine, our programme was taking shape nicely, and it was tempting simply to run a series of such interviews, bracketed with scornful remarks or parody from our production team, thus providing a kind of supermarket-tabloid thrill, using the abductees as fodder for mirth. It was certainly going to be hard for us to keep some sense of observation or opinion out of our piece, but we did feel there were serious issues that could be addressed in the midst of all this bewildering stuff.

As so many people were claiming to have had experiences with aliens, one of the questions we felt bound to ask was whether holding such beliefs was likely to do them any harm.

My old friend Dr Ian Miller — who I worked with on the Kurt Saxon story — was intrigued enough in our project to listen to some of the stories the abductees had told us and then make some general observations. 'There's quite a continuum,' he told us, 'from the harmless and minor delusions to the serious and bizarre. This alien abduction thing sometimes, of course, is a harmless belief, but there are others for whom the strong adherence to such views may in fact presage quite serious mental illness.'

During our interview with Miller, my mind raced over stories we'd covered of people with schizophrenia or manic depression who had committed quite serious crimes while suffering from delusions about microchips having been inserted in their heads, or the TV set in their front room being a receptor for messages from outer space. We'd covered more than one tale where people convinced of such things had taken their own lives or the lives of others. Hardly harmless stuff.

A bit of background checking on our abductees satisfied us there weren't any closet axe murderers among them. About the worst you could accuse any of these people of being was a little eccentric and somewhat larger than life. One of the group, a fashion-clothing cutter called Glen, really made our eyes glaze over.

Glen seemed to be the most steadfast believer of the lot, and his intense eyes and manner were accentuated by one of the most spectacular bouffant hairdos we'd ever seen on a male. He was absolutely sure great blocks of his life were disappearing into thin air as he found himself driving, in a trancelike state, across great tracts of the Auckland area to keep appointments with aliens who were drawing him into their clutches.

Glen would find himself, for no apparent reason, standing beside an open country field, from where he would be transported by light-speed aliens into their ships for a fresh encounter. His appointments with small greys were just like Syd's — for the purpose of taking his semen for intergalactic reproduction.

'You must ask yourself,' we tried to probe, 'why you, a humble clothing cutter from Glenfield, have been chosen as some kind of cosmic stud?'

A slight laugh from Glen, and then a bit of self-deprecation. 'No, it's not only me, there are hundreds of thousands of others to whom this is happening. I think the selection process, as it's been explained to me, is that they go for people who can feel emotion, and express that emotion, because they need that as quickly as possible, in terms of the breeding programme.'

Nagged, of course, by the many questions that scream out to be asked once you look into these stories, we worked our way through some of the most obvious ones with the abductees. To Syd, the supermarket guy:

'Surely your wife, Karen, who sleeps in the same bed as you, must notice, even on some occasions, that you have physically been transported out of the bed. She must know some of those occasions on which you've gone, and be able to verify your story?'

Syd shook his head patiently. 'No, you see, what happens is that if you're in a relationship with somebody, the aliens make sure that everybody in the house that's with you is "shut down" — even your pets, they're shut down. They get paralysed and you get taken; it's more of a deep sleep, actually.'

Next question. How come, we asked, with all those trips to the alien operating theatre, no one has brought back a single verifiable memento of their cosmic surgery?

Syd answers without hesitation. 'Think about a normal operation here on earth. You go into an operating room and have surgery done on you; there's no way you're gonna wake up once you're anaesthetised and grab something — you know what I mean?'

Iris chimed in quickly. 'You know I've been in those ships and in the theatres so often, and I've been lying there helpless, paralysed, thinking to myself I'd love to grab something, I'd love nothing more than to be able to grab a piece of that equipment to bring back and show somebody, but you can't, it's hopeless.'

There were endless potential follow-up questions, but this was the one that came to mind for me. 'Iris,' I asked carefully so as not to give offence, 'when I go to bed I generally get a good uninterrupted sleep, but you go to bed and at night you're abducted by aliens, probed, impregnated and subjected to visits to alien baby nurseries. How on earth do you go back to work the next day after an experience like that and simply behave normally?'

Iris thought for a moment and then gave the most stunningly down-to-earth answer we'd heard during the making of the programme. 'Well, you've got to get on with your life; you can't curl up in a ball and die. You've got to make the best of it. I often say I'm not a strange person — I'm an ordinary person who has strange things happen to her.'

Depending on whose journal or theory you're reading, explanations abound. Feelings of being trapped or held down, we are told — even real perceptions of pain — probably arise from a form of so-called sleep paralysis, from which we all suffer on occasion. The other deal, of course, may purely be an overdeveloped and colourful imagination.

Even Syd had to acknowledge, when we got down to the nitty-gritty, that he was still open to the possibility that one day somebody might be able to convince him that all the things he reckoned had happened to him were simply figments of a vivid imagination. For the moment, he pointed to the bruises and scars on his arm and said he was still steadfastly of the opinion that aliens were actively involved in his life.

Dr Miller was of the opinion that the beliefs of most of the people we'd interviewed would remain relatively harmless. Thinking this through, it occurred to me it was not unreasonable to draw comparisons between what abductees believe and the tenets of some religious groups. Both, after all, place major reliance on a range of matters that remain unseen and therefore unproveable.

One of the last acts in our alien drama occurred when we took Iris, at our suggestion, to meet an Auckland hypnotist to see whether, under his guidance, she could recover any more memories of the things she said she regularly experienced.

We undertook the experiment with somewhat mixed feelings — keen to see whether we could find support for any of Iris's stories, but aware of the controversy that surrounds hypnosis, even when performed by experts, because of its potential to implant memories that weren't there in the first place. Indeed, what worries some psychologists is that hypnosis — one of the techniques most widely employed by abduction investigators in the US — may do more harm than good when carried out on a person over a long period of time.

Iris underwent her hypnosis on a warm spring afternoon in the offices of a fairly well-known Auckland practitioner. Almost immediately she grew uncomfortable, speaking about where 'they're taking me'.

'And where is that?' asked the hypnotist.

'Where they always take me — to the room.' By now Iris was moving her head from side to side with a degree of agitation. This was a trance with some real terror.

'And what do they do to you there?' he asked gently.

'Awful, awful things!' Iris gasped.

'You tell me,' he went on.

'They always hurt you. It wouldn't be so bad if it didn't always hurt you, they poke you with their fingers. Ahhh! Ouch! When I ask them to stop they behave as if I'm not there.'

Shortly after saying this, Iris, gripping the arms of the chair in which she had slumped, did seem to be suffering from the sense that she was being molested by someone or something in a way that was deeply distressing. Coming out of the hypnosis she appeared OK, and as convinced as ever that she was indeed the regular victim of unwanted attention by people from beyond this planet.

Interestingly enough, a consistent theme in our interviews with abductees was that in no way did they wish to be pitied. They weren't looking for sympathy, nor did they necessarily ask to be believed: they simply wanted to be treated with a degree of dignity over matters they raised neither hysterically nor lightly — matters that played a large part in their lives and perceived experience.

The story we ultimately produced was, predictably, one of *Assignment*'s better-rating episodes of the year, and, I felt in hindsight, a valid journalistic exercise. It was hardly Pulitzer Prize territory but kept a team of us engrossed during the spring of 1995. *The X-Files* went on to enjoy popular acclaim for many more seasons, and fascination all over the world with the broader realms of the series' subject matter shows no signs of diminishing in the 21st century.

A big reality check for us was the realisation that not only alien abductees appear prone to vivid imaginings. Society in general — including journalists — are capable of taking even a sniff of the prospect of alien visitation and going wild. A search of TV and newspaper archives reminded me of a summer back in the late 1970s when New Zealand as a whole was gripped by the notion that little green men had arrived and had chosen as a 'hovering ground' — of all places — Kaikoura.

The craze began when the crew of a southbound cargo plane — a lumbering old thing called an Argosy — reported lights over the region that had no conventional explanation. Lights that appeared and then flashed away at colossal speed — just like Steven

Spielberg had shown us they could.

Everyone from locals with telescopes to visiting international TV crews who rode along on Argosy flights tracked the lights for a week or so, and to watch the TV news on a couple of nights was unavoidably to conclude there were many believers.

'It was an amazing time,' remembers evening news bulletin editor Chris Mitson. 'Yeah, I do recall the one night when we devoted virtually all of a half-hour news show to interviewing people who'd been tracking the lights. The possibility of alien visitation was a fairly intense thing.'

Even the Royal New Zealand Air Force became involved, sending up an Orion aircraft from its Whenuapai base to take a look. The results — inconclusive. Then one evening, as suddenly as they had arrived, the lights over Kaikoura disappeared. There were muttered attempts at explanation by the experts — something about the Moon or Venus and inversion layers or whatever — and when it was all over there was an almost tangible sense of national disappointment.

Chris Mitson reflected on the summer of lights: 'To me it was quite fascinating. When I thought about it later, it was almost like we had been living smugly in an era when we had decided, many of us, that there was no such thing as God, and we were doing OK now in our little corner of the galaxy. And when these lights came along, perhaps we suddenly realised how really alone we are in the vast universe, and how nice it would be to discover we had neighbours.'

In the final part of the eventual one-hour treatment of this subject, we dropped in on one last group of people — a group that manages to combine religion and aliens in a neat package. The Church of the Aetherius Society met in a converted suburban home on Auckland's North Shore with all of the solemnity of a conservative and long-standing faith. Our visit came 24 hours before an important event in the church's calendar: aliens were expected the very next day. It was, in the church's terminology, the eve of a big 'spiritual push'.

'We send our love and thankfulness,' said the Reverend Frank McManus, in sepulchral tones, as they all prayed, 'to the great cosmic beings on Satellite Number Three, which will be in orbit over the earth at noon tomorrow.'

The quietly spoken robed ones told me the ship was coming from Mars and would send down rays of positive energy that would help the earth during its visit.

Satellite Number Three, it transpired, was four kilometres long and carried extremely sophisticated equipment. The Reverend Margaret Kilbey explained it to me, her voice betraying barely suppressed excitement.

'This gear is so advanced it can pick out one person in an entire crowd and focus the beam on them.'

Time for another dumb question, I felt.

'These guys in the ship, they're from Mars, right?'

'Of course,' I was told.

'I've always wondered — how would any living, breathing thing survive on Mars. It's so cold and there's no breathable air.'

Margaret gave me the same sort of kindly smile I'd received when I'd first asked about the small greys.

'It's simple,' they told me. 'They live underground.'

At the very least, covering this story forced me to ask a couple of astronomers some hard questions about the physical realities of extraterrestrials and UFOs. Almost uniformly, the scientific types are of the view that we stand very little chance of making meaningful contact with beings on the other side of even our own small corner of space.

Why? Because even if any message they send us gets here at light speed, it will probably have left Planet Z a thousand years ago. By the time we decipher it — assuming we are able to — and send back our response, the initiators of the greeting will be long dead. Add to that the seeming impossibility of light-speed travel, and the fact that 'beaming up Scotty' would require harnessing the power of more electrons than actually exist in the entire universe, and it seems that to boldly go where no man has gone before may have to be confined to our dreams and TV dramas.

Darn it.

UPDATE

We lost touch with the abductees' support group for several years. However, when director Brett Cammell and I embarked on a documentary called 'Desperate Remedies' — an hour-long piece about people who search out alternative forms of treatment for cancer — it turned out one of the more radical clinics in town was being run by our old mate Glen — the abductee who used to get whisked down the Southern Motorway for alien sperm-snatching encounters in the green hills of Clevedon.

Glen was running something called the Rife Therapy Clinic — a place where people with cancer could go to sit among high-frequency glowing tubes that were supposed to disrupt a tumour and put them right. Business, in a big old house near Albany, was booming on the days we visited. Patients, some looking extremely sick, sat among the tubes; others soaked their feet in tubs of water with fizzing electrodes. In the basement, a woman with a tumour in her neck climbed into a hyperbaric oxygen chamber — therapy she preferred over surgery.

Glen, as intense as ever, could spare only a few minutes between consultations. It came as no surprise that several members of the abductees' support group, including Glen's cousin, Robert, and Iris, dropped in while we were there.

Glen told us he was being abducted a little less often these days, but he was still adamant, five years later, that it had indeed happened — he hadn't just imagined it. 'It was perhaps a season when they needed me a bit more, back then. It's been a little less frequent lately.'

Furthermore, he didn't feel being taken away by the small greys from time to time made him any less stable, or less effective as a therapist helping people with complex problems like terminal cancer. And I was convinced he believed that to his very core.

5

WEST SIDE STORY

It's hard to know what the illustrious New Zealand racing driver Bruce McLaren would have made of the street in West Auckland that bears his name. Bruce McLaren Road, in the suburb of Henderson, takes traffic from a busy industrial zone to an area of long-established fruit orchards. It's one of those 'nothing' streets you could drive up a thousand times and never be aware of its name.

Bruce McLaren Road became an intriguing part of my life in mid-1997 as I worked on a documentary we eventually called 'West Side Story', which examined one of the more mind-bending murders ever committed in this country, and its bizarre sequel.

For a number of years now, the people who live and work in streets like Bruce McLaren Road have worn a label — sometimes derisory, sometimes half-affectionate. They are 'Westies', a tag which, to those who use it sneeringly, denotes V8-driving, black-clad, usually long-haired male youths who generally wear their lack of sophistication as a badge of honour. Westie women (more commonly known as chicks) are regarded as similarly lower-class, and are usually written up as gum-chewing exponents of poor grammar with bad taste in clothing.

I should declare at this point that I've lived in West Auckland myself for most of my married life, and although I have a propensity for driving cars with between six and eight cylinders and my taste in popular music doesn't get much past the Who and the

Rolling Stones, I find the Westie stereotype a woefully inadequate basket for the incredibly rich and diverse cultures and people of one of New Zealand's most vibrant regions.

Cue, at this point, loud guffaws from my friends.

But seriously, I was among those died-in-the-wool Westies who bridled with a certain amount of indignation when, in the middle of 1997, an article appeared in the *New Zealand Herald* that drew what to many minds were far-reaching conclusions about the nature of the district and its people from one particularly disturbing case of homicide.

However, one has to acknowledge that as the case of the so-called Body in the Boot affair unfolded before a jury in the Auckland High Court in the winter of that year, it was hard not to gasp at what Jason Menzies was accused of doing to his de facto wife, Stephanie Skidmore. Menzies was alleged to have strangled Stephanie, and then to have left her body to decompose, first in their flat at 80J Bruce McLaren Road, and later, for several weeks, in the boot of his old Falcon car outside the apartment complex.

To make matters worse, Menzies was also accused of having lied when interviewed for a TV programme about Stephanie's disappearance. He told the police, and then TV interviewers, that she had run away. He asked publicly for her to come home to him and their two-year-old daughter, Alexis.

It was eerie looking back at the television news pictures from the time of Stephanie's disappearance. There is the somewhat gothic-looking Menzies playing with Alexis on the deck of his parents' home, looking every bit the anxious partner, desperate to know the whereabouts of his woman.

Perhaps a seasoned observer of human behaviour could have picked up, even back then, that there was way more to this story than just a woman who'd apparently taken off. The images from the evening news of June 1996 show Menzies, his hand never far from his mouth, looking furtively to one side and unable to meet the interviewer's gaze, saying Stephanie had told him she was leaving and it was now over to him to look after their daughter. Menzies' mum, Sandra, mercifully unaware of the true horror of what had unfolded, also went on television to appeal to Stephanie to come home.

'We want to know you're OK, Stephanie. Please call us and let us know,' she urged.

When the truth eventually came out, it was truly shocking. After an argument between the volatile couple on Mother's Day 1996, Menzies had choked Stephanie nearly to death in the Bruce McLaren Road flat, then finished her off with a length of electrical cord round the neck.

But that was only part of the case against Menzies. As we began piecing together material for a one-hour programme on the murder, we learned of decisions made by a group of young West Auckland men that almost defied imagination.

In TV news and current affairs, it's the journo who usually gets the credit if a story is any good. But so often the hard yards are done by a researcher, whose name appears briefly in relatively small type among the credits at the end of the show. This story was no exception. A hard-working, genial young woman called Jane Skinner, our *Assignment* researcher, was in every sense the advance guard on this story: she ventured into the lives of Jason Menzies' mates and got them talking. From then on it was relatively easy.

One of the first interviews Jane set up was with a young man called Danny Howe. He looked remarkably like Menzies — the trademark black clothing, long hair and pasty complexion. But, as we spoke together in the tidy front room of a Titirangi home Danny shared with his girlfriend, he also exuded a kind of laid-back charm.

'Jason told us he'd done something pretty wrong. We didn't know what to expect when we got there,' Danny reflected. 'He rang me up and showed me where she was — lying there in the bedroom — but by then it was too late.' Danny and another mate, Bronson Legge, had stood in the doorway to the second bedroom at 80J Bruce McLaren Road and contemplated what their buddy had done. Stephanie's body had been there for a couple of hours and no one was sure what to do. Going to the police, it seemed, was not an option.

At this point Danny stepped squarely into the middle of Jason Menzies' nightmare: Menzies urged him to come and stay in the flat with him.

People would later say Menzies was a rather naïve young man, but he'd had the presence of mind to change the rental agreement for the flat into his name and remove money from Stephanie's bank account by the time Danny moved in, a couple of days after the murder. Two-year-old Alexis was being cared for part time by Menzies' parents, who lived a couple of kilometres away, but was also spending a good deal of time at the flat where, if you can believe it, Stephanie's body continued to lie on the floor of the bedroom.

Our interview with Danny gave us the feeling he'd had the benefit of several months to think about how to present his part in the unfolding horror story. He'd also received a let-off in return for his testimony. Nevertheless, when I questioned him he spoke matter-of-factly.

'So, at the time you moved into the flat, where was Stephanie?' I asked.

'She was still there, yeah, on the floor. There was a bit of a debate as to whether I was going to move in, but Jason sort of forced me really.'

'So when you moved into the flat her body was still lying on the bedroom floor?'

'Yep.'

'About ten days after she'd been murdered?'

'Yep, that's right.'

It's hard to know exactly what to expect when you conduct such an interview; maybe, at least, some tears, some indication of remorse. Danny seemed to have dealt with the whole ordeal fairly well.

Bronson Legge, another Menzies lookalike, was similarly low-key in his interview. 'Yeah, we went into the bedroom, looked at her on the floor and kind of freaked out.'

'Did either of you think about going to the police?' I inquired.

'Yeah, that was going through everyone's minds, but I think we were all quite scared, you know.'

Reeling a little from such candour, we went to the flat at Bruce McLaren Road one evening to get some sense of the physical environment in which everything had taken place. The large building houses mostly commercial premises on the ground floor, with a few flats above. We had been anticipating a real dump, but as we climbed the stairs to the door of 80J, we discovered a complex in remarkably good repair — spacious and comfortable even.

The then tenants were intrigued enough to allow us about half an hour to look round the large flat — somewhat tidied up — to take pictures and to record some links. I stood in the front room and tried to imagine the scene there the year before. The sounds of a martial arts class in full cry drifted up from the floor below.

As we wandered from room to room, we sought the feeling of a home in which a woman who'd been dead 10 days lay on the floor in one room, while two young men, Jason and Danny, slept in adjoining rooms, and during which time a bright-eyed toddler had obviously wandered between the living and the dead, no doubt more than a little perplexed at the fact that her mother was motionless, not to mention decomposing.

Such strange behaviour must have been caused by something in the water at this place, we thought. The carpet on which Stephanie's body had lain had been replaced. The tenants knew full well they were living in a flat with a ghastly reputation, but seemed remarkably unconcerned. 'Bloody mad Westies,' I think my director, Brett Cammell, muttered, trying his best to get a rise out of me. As I recall, I refused to take the bait.

We walked back down the stairs and tried to recreate in our minds the scene that had unfolded a few days after Danny had moved in, as he and Menzies, under cover of darkness, had wrapped up Stephanie's body and prepared to take it to another location.

'So obviously people who were listening to you in court, and who are watching this interview now,' I said to Danny, 'are shaking their heads, for a start, and asking how you could move into a flat in which there was a woman's dead body lying on the floor.'

For perhaps the first time, a flicker of reflection appeared in Danny's eyes as he remarked, 'Yeah, silly thing to do I suppose — I guess it was just over friendship.' My own eyes at this point moved slightly to Danny's left, to where his girlfriend, Tracey, was sitting, listening to the interview. From her, no trace of anxiety or sense of blame; if anything, a look of quite genuine sympathy for her boyfriend, of whom she clearly had no fear. This was a young woman who obviously understood the principle of 'mateship', which had driven a young man to prefer the notion of supporting his friend over going to the authorities and getting this hideous matter sorted out. Danny took up the story about moving Stephanie's body.

'I'd had quite a bit to drink the night we had to do it — or the night he wanted us to do it — and once you're in that state of drunkenness nothing matters. And after I'd come home he forced me, or asked me several times, to do it. I was gonna leave but I decided to help him because we'd been through heaps together, and I didn't want to break our friendship up. So stupid me did it.'

Things then got quiet as Danny described how Menzies had 'got everything ready' and, with the pair of them freaking out, they'd carried Stephanie's body downstairs and placed it in the boot of one of a number of old cars Menzies had parked outside the apartment complex.

There the body was to stay for seven weeks, as the police and public laboured under the misapprehension that Stephanie was still alive and somewhere out there — in suburban Auckland, perhaps. Danny and Bronson helped keep the secret, which took a toll on Menzies in particular, as he became increasingly agitated and 'stressed out over the secret they were all carrying'.

On 28 June 1996, police executed a search warrant on 80J Bruce McLaren Road, and also on Menzies' Falcon. The autopsy photographs show what was recovered from the boot of the car. It barely resembled a human being. Menzies was arrested and charged with murder. Among those most devastated by the news of his arrest were his parents, Grayson and Sandra Menzies, whom we interviewed in their tidy suburban home in Glen Eden. Still fresh in Sandra's mind was the TV interview she'd granted only a couple of weeks earlier, in which she'd pleaded Stephanie to come home. Now she realised her son had been hiding a devastating secret from her the whole time.

There are times in journalism when you feel an enormous sorrow for the people you're interviewing. In conversation with Grayson and Sandra one evening, I had one of those moments. As Alexis, then in their care, played at their feet, I glanced at a couple of framed portraits of their son and Stephanie in happier times. As the interview progressed it became clear I was talking to a regular couple who'd had the same dreams for their kids as anyone might have. Their son's actions were as incomprehensible to them as to everyone else.

'When I asked "Why did you leave the body there?"' Grayson told me, 'Jason said, "Well, what was I to do? There was nothing I could do, and I wanted to be with Lexi for as long as possible. They wouldn't believe me anyway." That's what he told me when it was all over.'

Said Sandra: 'I know what happened now; he just froze, and I told him, "Jason, I wish you had come to me and your father."' She sat in her lounge that evening with a somewhat hunted look in her eyes, wondering what would become of the son she regarded as little more than a boy, now sitting in a prison cell.

There were visual metaphors aplenty as the trial got under way: the poignant sight of Stephanie's American-based mother as she entered the hearing, surrounded by well-groomed friends trying to help her keep her composure, contrasted sharply with the rough-and-ready, long-haired friends of Jason Menzies, who seemed to wear only blank and diffident stares as they walked in and out of the Auckland High Court, hands thrust deep into the pockets of denim jackets or black jeans.

As the case was outlined to the jury, it was easy to portray Menzies as a heartless villain. He had taken his partner's life, he had lied, he had been extremely manipulative, and he had dragged his friends into a distasteful conspiracy. The jury had little difficulty finding him guilty of murder.

As Menzies began his life sentence, a feature in the *New Zealand Herald* rang out with sombre observations of the world in which he and his friends lived. Journalist Carroll du Chateau, in a piece entitled 'The Body in the Boot', made some compelling observations. 'Menzies and his friends,' she said, 'had slipped into a subculture that is still depressingly common.' These young men inhabited 'a world of unemployment, dope smoking and worse, where cars are more important than women and kids, and mates mean more than both.' Du Chateau went on to write about 'pockets of low life such as those inhabited by Menzies and Howe'.

It wasn't the first time Carroll and I had found our lives intersecting on West Auckland stories: nine years earlier we had both covered the trial of a couple of thugs accused of beating to death a farmer from the rural part of Auckland's west after a minor traffic accident. Carroll harked back to her earlier piece, which she'd entitled 'The Mudguard Murder', in this latest, very strong article about the neighbourhood.

I met Carroll for coffee in West Auckland while we were constructing our documentary, and asked whether in hindsight her strongly worded article had given her any cause for second thought. 'As a journalist you have to be a little bit brave,' she told me. 'You can't water things down to be politically correct, and I think you'd have to agree that what they did was pretty low — they certainly didn't live their lives at what you would call a high level.'

A number of people in West Auckland were stung by her article — not least, the colourful and outspoken mayor, Bob Harvey. They were hurt by what they felt were unfair generalisations about the area they lived in. But there were also those — friends of both Jason Menzies and Stephanie Skidmore — who felt media coverage of the trial, including Carroll's 'Body in the Boot' article, had overlooked some realities of the couple's relationship and of the crime itself.

Stephanie, it seemed from many conversations we had during our research, had been a very violent and temperamental young woman, who, having earned a living as a stripper and a prostitute in Auckland's red light district, had been more than Menzies, a quietly spoken young boy from West Auckland, had been capable of handling. This posed a considerable dilemma to us as programme makers.

One is loathe, even in vigorous journalism, to speak ill of the dead, and it was with a little trepidation that we ventured into this territory. Nevertheless, in reporting the opinions of a range of people about the young couple, we did discover how tempestuous their relationship had been in the lead-up to the awful events of Mother's Day 1996. It turned out Stephanie had barely been in her teens when she'd started inhabiting a twilight world.

When she finally met the shy young Glen Eden boy, it was scarcely going to be a match made in heaven, even though the couple shared parenthood of a little girl. Friends noticed that, from very early in the relationship, Stephanie was prone to flying into almost uncontrollable rages, in which she quite severely beat her partner.

Friend Linda Exler recalled standing next to the couple in the middle of Auckland's Queen Street one night when Stephanie completely 'lost it' and delivered Menzies 'a real hiding', quite oblivious to passers-by. 'I was standing right there when it happened,' said Linda. 'She was punching him, kicking him, grabbing handfuls of his hair, and he just stood there and took it. All he could say was "Get her off me, please, get her off me," and four of us friends were standing around watching this. I don't think any of us were game to get involved in the middle of that — she was completely out of control.'

When Menzies ultimately appeared in court and declared Stephanie had attacked him with a knife and that he'd acted in self-defence, his claim was rubbished by the prosecution as being 'not within a bull's roar of the truth'.

Another friend of the couple, Kim Burns, told our programme she had been witness to a number of violent incidents involving the couple, including one in which Stephanie had threatened Menzies with a knife and he'd asked her insistently to put it away.

Of course, by the time the case got to court, who was going to give much credence to the word of a young man who'd behaved in such an outrageous manner towards his partner's body? This was where the whole business started to appear so tragic. Here was a very unsophisticated man, who'd had little in the way of brushes with the law apart from driving offences, who apparently hatched plans for a corpse that made little or no sense.

From prison, Menzies would tell Kim that Stephanie had attacked him in the Mother's Day incident: she had deadlocked the door, put the key down her blouse and come at him with a knife. He had then put the young woman in a 'choker hold' to calm her down and had obviously gone too far. Kim was inclined to believe this, because she and the others we spoke to had never seen Menzies be physically violent towards Stephanie — on the contrary, he'd seemed just to take the beatings she'd dished out.

Journalistically, of course, this was incredibly hard for us to assess: the perpetrator was in prison, and inaccessible to us; it was obviously in his personal interests to maintain a story of lesser culpability; and Stephanie's version of events had died with her. It seemed to be one of those stories for which we'd be damned whatever we reported.

We braced ourselves for the mail bag we'd get for possibly appearing to suggest Stephanie had brought the awful things that had happened upon her own head — which was not our aim. What's more, having changed the name on the rental agreement, left Stephanie's body to rot and withdrawn money from Stephanie's bank account, Menzies gave an observer serious cause to wonder whether he might have been quite as naïve and gullible as his friends were suggesting.

We decided to forge ahead with the story in any case, because it was one of those tales that had so much 'gosh factor' we felt compelled to try and tell it any way we could.

This was evidently also part of what fascinated Carroll du Chateau in the writing of her 'Body in the Boot' piece. She had been trying to delve a little deeper into the psyche of the neighbourhoods in which Jason Menzies, Danny Howe and Bronson Legge had grown up, suggesting there might be something seriously amiss if men could behave so repugnantly and have such a fractured view of life and death.

'You can't go round murdering people and leaving their body on the floor of a flat and then putting it in the boot of a car simply because you're too shy to tell anybody,' said Carroll during our interview. 'Sure it was irrational, but there's more to it than that. It was an atrocity. There's no excuse for that.' A quite neat encapsulation of the central issue, I thought.

Our interview with Danny Howe revealed a strong sense of indignation at having been labelled a 'low life' — even though he now admitted helping Jason dispose of Stephanie's body was, 'the dumbest thing I ever did'. To Danny's own amazement, he was never charged with any offence related to the affair.

'During the court testimony and in subsequent newspaper articles you were portrayed as a real animal, weren't you?' I asked him, straight out.

'We were just dragged into it, me, Bronson and another guy. We didn't know what to do.' And then, in a bit of ironical self-deprecation, he added, 'There's no way that every Westie's like that.'

A somewhat strange admission, we observed in the documentary; a bit like saying, 'Sure, I may have done something dumb, but don't think you can label all my friends in this neighbourhood the same way!' Again, I glanced at Danny's partner, Tracey, who stuck by him, regardless.

'To me they're talking about someone completely different to the guy I know,' she said. 'To me he's dependable, treats me like an angel. I've never been treated this good, basically. Danny's very helpful with my son, will often pick him up from school, not aggressive at all, not the person that they've been portraying in the article.'

'But he valued friendship more than his responsibility to reveal the fact that a hideous crime had been committed,' I said gently.

Tracey thought for a moment. 'Putting all this aside, I have absolutely no fear of Danny.'

We knew anyone watching our programme would quickly reach the conclusion that many of the people we'd interviewed found the repairing of injured reputations more important than an honest confrontation of what had been a horrible crime. There'd be no escaping that.

Jason's own parents, although horrified at what their son had done with Stephanie's body after she'd died, reflected with some sympathy on his earnest assertion that he didn't feel he was a murderer. But by then, of course, it was all too late. Here was another family, desperately trying to figure out how a loved one's life could have gone so completely off the rails.

Towards the end of our filming schedule, we spent some time with Sandra and Grayson Menzies in a playground near where their son had grown up, as they watched little Alexis at play. At this stage Alexis was in their care, but a day of reckoning was coming on this matter, too.

Stephanie's mother was working hard to gain custody of the girl. Sandra and Grayson's view was that because Alexis had spent so much time in their care during her parents' rocky relationship, they were the natural choice to look after her now her mother was dead and her father would be serving a long stretch in prison.

Perhaps not surprisingly, this was to become one of the most contentious parts of our documentary. Very strong feelings were aroused over the fact that the little girl had been shown in it. It was suggested that it was inappropriate for one so young, and in such a vulnerable situation, to be part of a high-profile television programme.

The Broadcasting Standards Authority looked closely at strong complaints about our programme, and although it declined to uphold the complaints, it signalled that in future it would take a strong view on television coverage of children in contentious situations.

In the event, the Family Court ruled in favour of Stephanie Skidmore's mother, and Alexis was ultimately placed in her care. Grayson and Sandra were predictably devastated.

All terribly tragic — and we were left with the gnawing conclusion at the back of our minds that although Menzies had done something rotten, there was every chance that if he hadn't crossed paths with Stephanie, he'd have gone on to lead a relatively uneventful life. No denying it, however: when the chips were down, he and his mates had behaved unspeakably.

As for Danny Howe and Bronson Legge, who kept the awful secret for so long, our last contact with them was as they jammed away on their guitars in the basement of Danny's house. Bronson had written a song about the flat in Bruce McLaren Road entitled, simply, '80J'. It was a dark, brooding piece of heavy metal — a work in progress, as they say; still waiting on some words.

Danny confessed he still thought about Stephanie quite a lot. 'You know,' he said, with perhaps more animation than he showed at any other time that day, 'I guess I prayed at one stage, spoke to her and said I hope she didn't hate Jason for what he'd done to her. I said, "I hope you don't hate me too, just rest in peace."'

In our documentary we tried to get underneath the skin of the West Auckland communities Danny Howe, Bronson Legge and Jason Menzies called home. In the end, no compelling statistics came to light indicating a hugely greater incidence of violent crime in those neighbourhoods than in other low- to middle-income parts of Auckland. Indeed, crime had actually been trending down a little around the time of Stephanie's death. Menzies' home had been loving and average; Menzies himself had had a job, had had no problems with alcohol and hadn't led a life of crime. He had lacked social competence, had lost his temper in a most violent way, and had had no experience to prepare him for the consequences of such an awful act. To meet his mum and dad is to shake your head and simply want to share their grief and profound confusion.

And so, what of West Auckland?

A common temptation in journalism is to engage in caricature and stereotype, and to add a dash of intellectual or moral superiority for good measure. 'Westie', we ultimately found, was as inadequate a label as any other pejorative term applied to a neighbourhood or social group. It would be as easy to point out that, per head of population, back at the time of the 1984 Olympic Games, West Auckland produced more gold-medal-winning athletes than any other spot in the world; that it has been the cradle of more great rugby and league players than any place of similar size; or that it has the country's most stunning beaches and produces some of its best wines.

But then, I suppose I would say that, wouldn't I?

6

IN MEMORY OF ANDREW

Andrew and Kate Dominikovich looked for all the world like the happiest couple alive. When they strolled into the foyer of the home I was visiting in Lower Hutt about five years ago, they both had wide grins, and perched on Andrew's shoulders was a lovely fair-haired boy called Josh, at that stage barely a year old. Kate and Andrew were friends of my associate producer, Linda Gollan, and they'd dropped in on the spur of the moment to say hi while we were on a shoot for another story.

'Kate's a medical rep and a mum,' Linda told me breezily, 'and Andrew's got a great new job as a doctor up at Hutt Hospital.' Kate was a short dynamo of a woman who exuded energy and a passion for life, while Andrew looked about as casual as an off-duty doctor could.

The couple were clearly enjoying the new challenges of parent-hood, and from our conversation it seemed Andrew's job as house surgeon, while stretching, was proving to be everything he'd dreamed of. It had taken the young man many years of sweat and hard work to make the leap from medical technician to fully-fledged doctor, but he was finally at the point, it appeared, where his dream of practising medicine was being realised.

Like many people one meets, Kate and Andrew were stored in my short-to-mid-term memory banks, and I didn't give them another thought until Linda called me just before Christmas about a year later. Her news was among the most ghastly tidings imaginable. While on a business trip to Auckland, Kate had received the news that Andrew had been found dead in their Lower Hutt home. It was quite clear the 34-year-old doctor, father and husband had taken his own life. The funeral was to be in a few days' time.

You always shake your head when you hear about suicide, but this one had me especially foxed. The guy had seemed so darned happy and relaxed. How could he leave behind a wonderful woman like Kate and a two-year-old boy? And then Linda fed me another tragic detail: Kate thought she might be pregnant. If that was true, Andrew had died not knowing he was to be a father again.

There are some blurry lines in journalism and film-making, no matter what people tell you. While I was driving to Wellington for the Christmas holidays, it occurred to me about halfway into the trip that a series Linda and I were making, about the role of faith in the lives of ordinary New Zealanders, could include no more potentially powerful a story than that of a Christian woman coming to terms with the death of a beloved husband.

Andrew had been an accomplished worship leader at his local Baptist church, and it was clear to me that the loss of this young man to his family, community, hospital and church was going to be a huge deal. Linda had already made an offer to Kate, on our company's behalf, to provide a professional cameraman to videotape the funeral. I now made a cellphone call to Linda that I knew might well be a test not only of our professional relationship, but also of her close friendship with Kate. 'How do you think Kate would react to an approach from us to tell her story over the next year or so?' I asked.

Linda thought long and hard, and eventually we agreed a personal approach to Kate by me, laying out our request in the most unthreatening way possible, would be the best way to proceed. This is hard territory; there are days when you wonder how much of a vulture you must appear when you raise with grieving people the prospect of their pain and sorrow becoming part of a television programme that will be viewed by hundreds of thousands of people.

Sometimes I have to ask myself how I would react if I were on the phone dealing with such a request from a journalist. Hard and pragmatic as I have become over the years, I really don't know how I'd respond if it were my own wife or kids who were involved. Kate was gracious enough to agree to see me early in the New Year, with Andrew's death only a matter of weeks behind her.

It was bucketing down on the afternoon I sat with Kate in her small kitchen, talking about wounds that still ran incredibly deep. She told me it was possible to categorise her days on a scale of 1 to 10, with 1 for really low and 10 for great — but that there were some days she could only call a minus 15.

A former nurse, Kate managed to keep sufficient composure that day to take me through the events of the week when she'd travelled to Auckland, with Josh, and how she'd got the news she no longer had a husband.

'I was up in the office at work, and one of the managers said, "The police are looking for you, I don't know what it's about; might just be a speeding ticket or whatever." I thought, I don't remember speeding, and was quite light-hearted about that for a moment, but why would the police want to come and actually give me a ticket? I never imagined it could have anything to do with Andrew; it never entered my thoughts.'

When the news finally came through to her, she said, the phone felt like lead in her hands. 'When they told me, I didn't want to believe it, as you don't. You want them to be horribly wrong; you want them to have identified the wrong person. So I quickly phoned home to make sure they had identified the wrong guy. There was no answer — the phone kept ringing, and it sort of hit home in a major blow. My initial thought was Josh, my little boy, my little darling who Daddy absolutely adored, wasn't going to have a daddy any more.'

Raindrops that seemed ridiculously big rolled down the window as I sat for a moment and let that sink in. To my surprise, Kate readily agreed to be interviewed for our programme, and to allow us to document her journey over the next year or so, as she awaited the coroner's inquest into Andrew's death and learned about life as a widow.

As we began filming a couple of weeks later, the kind of deep frustration any observer would feel on hearing Andrew's story often surfaced among our crew as we tried desperately to make sense, for ourselves and for Kate, of what had happened. We watched the videos of the proud, beaming young man graduating from medical school and looking so pleased he'd finally earned the right to be called a doctor — and couldn't help wondering.

The Dominikovich family had moved to Lower Hutt when Josh was just four weeks old. Andrew had begun his job at Hutt Hospital, and eventually they'd bought a house not far from where he worked.

Kate recalled: 'When Andrew was doing the long hours just up the road at the hospital, it meant Josh and I could go up and see him. When he was doing an eight a.m. to midnight, which was all too often, we would go in and spend time with him. We knew how vital it was for us to have time together as a family, and for Andrew as a new dad.'

Any five minutes Kate could sneak into the hospital with Josh, she would go. 'I'd head over there with a picnic lunch or tea, wandering round the corridors from ward to ward so we could see him and chat to him. We'd make him cups of coffee and keep him awake.'

The family of three became quite a curiosity on the wards. Such devotion, people thought.

'I think his colleagues were always quite interested to know what I had in my basket. I got to know lots about him as a health professional during those visits. Andrew was always looking out for other people — he had such a soft heart. Anyone in need, his heart would turn to jelly; and he'd go to ridiculous lengths, even going round and doing the garden for one elderly man he'd discharged. I think Andrew had become quite a phenomenon after a short time.'

But the young doctor who'd started his medical career with such an open heart was also struggling with his own demons. For many years he'd fought awful depression, which could sneak up on him in most unpredictable ways and drive him to the point of absolute despair. Kate had known about Andrew's tendency to depression even before they were married, but she had determined in her heart she would stand by him and grant him the grace and the room to try to work things out. As it was, she said their marriage had been a very happy one despite Andrew's bouts of deep melancholy and depression.

'He was a gorgeous man,' Kate told me on that first day. 'That's one of the key words I use. Other words? I could say compassion-ate, sensitive, caring, creative, always on the lookout for other people, here to do a job and to do it well, a perfectionist. In many ways we were incredibly happy, and when we got to our first anni-versary I thought man, if that's hard, it's going to be such a cruise for the next fifty years. We had a great time, and as far as it being a big adjustment was concerned, it never felt like that. It was like moving in with your best friend, and we loved it. It was the right timing, a perfect match.'

But there was no denying it: life as a new house surgeon in a busy hospital brought stresses that would have tested the most stable personality. Towards the end of 1997, Andrew Domini-kovich's world started to unravel, as the pressure of the long hours and huge responsibilities he faced started to crowd in on him. He became unwell and very distracted.

The hospital granted him two weeks' sick leave. Kate recalled: 'I think we both felt the time off was going to do Andrew a lot of good, because he had started to stress out badly. But after two weeks he told me he didn't feel any different — and he felt like he should have, given that he'd supposedly been away from work pres-sures for a whole fortnight.'

So Andrew's sick leave was extended for two more weeks, but his anxiety didn't seem to abate. He told Kate he didn't feel bet-ter, and thought he would be going straight back into a work routine that might well prove too hard to handle.

Andrew got a medical certificate from his GP saying he was to go on to light duties to ease himself back into the hospital system. Whether this would be possible neither Andrew nor Kate were sure, because he was about to return to what was ordinarily a very busy shift pattern. Christmas and New Year were coming up, and with some of the other house surgeons away or sick, it looked as if Andrew might have to relieve for them.

Andrew had only been back at work for a couple of days when it became clear to Kate that the stress he'd felt under before going on leave had not abated and was, if anything, getting worse. He'd call her from the hospital, talking in almost panicked tones about how he wondered if he could cope with the jobs he was being given.

'Eventually he told me, "I'm going to be OK, I'm determined I'm going to do this, it's not going to get the better of me. I've had the leave, I'm going to give it my best shot." So he did.' However, he was far from winning his dreadful internal battle.

Andrew was at home, on his own, on the morning Kate was in Auckland on business. She had no premonition, or idea at all, that this was the day Andrew was to end his life. The discovery of his body at home was made by the pastor of the local Baptist church the Dominikovichs had been attending. Kate came back to Wellington and began the gut-wrenching process of arranging a funeral, and trying to explain to a two-year-old where Dad had gone.

On a rainy afternoon, Kate and Josh came to farewell Andrew at the Avalon Baptist Church, and reviewing the tapes of the funeral one sees a familiar pain. Suicides always bring out a huge range of conflicting emotions, and among the eulogies that day were a couple of tributes bordering on the angry.

So it was that a young mother, now pregnant with another child, said goodbye at a graveside and prepared to face a very new kind of life. As we began dropping in and out of Kate and Josh's life over the next few months, I found myself full of admiration for a woman who evidently had bone-deep convictions about herself, her faith and her ability to make a new start.

From the outset, she refused to allow herself to get bitter about what Andrew had done. She had a huge sense of appreciation of, and sympathy for, the terrible place he must have been at in his mind to have snapped that morning and taken his own life.

Kate determined that in dealing with Josh's questions she would always teach him that Andrew had been a hero. 'I'll always remind him of the wonderful daddy he had. The daddy that was a winner, that worked very hard and was someone to be proud of.'

On the day we began our filming with Kate, the sun streamed in to the little dining room in their house and Josh stood studiously nearby, listening carefully to our conversation. Moments later I saw him out in the back yard, wandering quite purposefully between the house and the fence with an old cellphone pressed to his ear.

Kate gave a thin smile and explained. 'Andrew used to call him quite a bit from the hospital right before Josh went to bed. He's been trying to phone Daddy a bit lately in the last couple of weeks, dialling heaven I guess, and saying, "Daddy, Daddy, hello?" and then he turns round to me and says, "Oh, Mum, he's not talking back," and then I have to explain to him that he's not going to be talking back — that Daddy's died and he hasn't got a phone with him — so Josh hangs up and says, "Oh, bye," quite happy to put that aside for a moment.

'There are times, though, when it does get a bit heartbreaking. He looked round the house for Andrew quite a bit in the first couple of weeks. Andrew often played hide-and-seek when he got home from work so Josh has gone to all those hiding places to see if Daddy is playing, and I've had to let him do it, then sat down quietly with him later and said, "You won't be able to find Daddy, he's not here."'

We wandered down to the local shopping mall later that morning, Josh charging on ahead then rushing back and asking for money for the Postman Pat car so he could ride and rollick for a while.

'What about the whole God and suicide deal?' I asked Kate. 'I mean, in many religions suicide's quite a no-no, isn't it? You and Andrew were people of quite strong faith. How have you dealt with some of those big questions?'

Kate was nodding even as I asked the question, and it was evident she'd done quite a bit of thinking on the subject already.

'Knowing who Andrew was and where his heart was, I don't see it as being very shameful. I know how instant the choice was — it wasn't premeditated, and who are we to judge other people for their sin or whatever? Who are we to say that it was the worst thing someone could do? I've now come to believe that we have a good God, who doesn't examine every act we do, as if He's peering at our lives under a microscope. I think God has a wide-angle lens on our lives and takes a very generous and loving view of everything we do, including our failures.'

As we sat at lunch in the mall, Kate explained she'd undertaken some quite deep prayer and had called out to God to help her get a sense of finality over Andrew's ultimate destiny.

'It was brilliant, really — it hit me the day after. It was like God was saying, you know, when Andrew got to those pearly gates, "Bad choice, Andrew, but your home's ready, your room's ready, welcome home, son."'

If Kate had any fears about the reaction of her and Andrew's friends to his suicide, and about their involvement in her life from then on, she was pleasantly surprised. Almost uniformly, people were understanding and supportive. One dear friend wrote a letter to Josh to be read when he's old enough to fully appreciate the course of his dad's life:

> Dear Joshua,
> You've got a wonderful Daddy who'll be watching you always now. Your Dad had real boldness. He knew what he'd been saved from, and wanted to tell the world. I hope one day you'll read this and hold your head high. Your Dad was a Dad to be proud of and one day if you run the race he faithfully ran, you'll meet him again and know that for yourself.

On the other side of the ledger, however, Kate found dealing with the social welfare system an incredible trial, often laced with almost unbelievable insensitivity.

'Going in and asking for a widow's benefit was obviously something I thought I'd never have to do, and it came especially hard for me because I've always been so self-reliant. Everything I've got I've worked for, and having to go into Income Support was very difficult.

'If you can believe it, I went in the day after I buried Andrew and one of the comments that sticks out is that they told me if Andrew hadn't died and they were to find out about it, then I would have to reimburse them for the benefit.'

I did a double take at that point. 'If they were to find out he hadn't really died?'

'Yeah,' said Kate with a wry smile. 'And I thought to myself I'd be *happy* to reimburse you the money — plus interest — if I found that out too. I had no idea there were those attitudes around — I'd heard it from others, but my experience was very tough. It's great that we've got the system that we can use for a period of time, but I didn't need to feel guilty about what had happened to my husband and I wasn't prepared to accept that. I thought they can take everything else away from me but they're not going to take away my dignity.'

At the outset of making the programme, I had made Kate an

offer I've made others trying to decide whether to commit to a documentary about a sensitive matter. I had told her that if we got a little way down the track and she decided she didn't want to proceed, we could drop the project. Here's the interesting thing: having said the same thing to about a dozen people in very highly charged stories, I have never once had anyone pull out. Trust grows up, and the person at the heart of the proposed documentary feels a kind of empowerment. By now, Kate was telling me and Linda she wanted to proceed; she really did think that telling her story would help other people.

Over the next few months, Kate waited expectantly for a call from the coroner's office — a call to say a date had been set to review the circumstances of Andrew's death. She was grateful the insurance company paid out on Andrew's policy — that was one hurdle fewer, one threat to her self-sufficiency she didn't have to face.

Nine months after Andrew had taken his life, there had still not been an inquest. We dropped in for another interview. Kate, almost ready to give birth, was hugely frustrated — there was no chance of complete emotional closure on the issue. The process was complicated by a police report on the case, which, when it arrived in her hands, Kate found to be riddled with inaccuracies. Usually strong these days, but suddenly on the verge of tears, Kate said with exasperation: 'How can I believe they've written down everything that's relevant when several of the key facts they've got here are completely wrong? I don't have any confidence in the process, and I can't afford to stop grieving before the inquest, because I know it's going to drag it all up again. I don't want the wound in my heart to heal totally, because I know it's going to be reopened when I have to go to see the coroner. But I'm ready for it all to be over.'

This was insight for me. Journalists live by a diary system — we shovel stuff mechanically into files, or into computer systems nowadays — and we often moan because a court case or inquest we're covering gets adjourned or delayed or postponed. We grizzle because the scheduling of judicial events doesn't suit our deadlines, or we beat the desk with frustration when a major criminal trial ends with a hung jury and we've suddenly lost the lead story from

101

that week's programme. For the Kates of this world, delays of this sort are not inconvenient, they are all-consuming. Passing story for me, real life for someone like Kate.

Later in September, Caleb Nathan Dominikovich arrived — a healthy eight-and-a-half-pound boy. Kate wasn't on her own for the birth — she had a wonderfully supportive midwife, and her great friend Sara Carey was there urging her on. To Kate, Caleb looked stunningly like Andrew, and the birth drew Kate and Josh together in powerful and delightful ways.

One afternoon, as we interviewed her, Kate was breast-feeding Caleb, and Joshua, still not yet three years old, carefully placed a dirty glass in the dishwasher. This was not for our benefit — he was completely domesticated.

'This little guy of mine has wisdom beyond his years, you know. He would come to Caleb as I was bathing him and say, "Don't worry, little fella, being a baby isn't so hard. I've been there, I know what it's like. You're going to make it!"'

'He obviously feels even as a two- to three-year-old that he has big shoes to fill, doesn't he?' I asked.

'Yeah, and it's gorgeous, it's in his nature,' Kate told me. 'He suddenly came out the other day with the idea of going up one of the posh streets around here and trying to find me a new husband. Josh reckons we should simply knock on some doors and ask if anyone has a nice man they don't want anymore.'

In many ways it was those around Kate who found this time especially poignant. Sara Carey told me as we sat on the back porch in Lower Hutt: 'I stayed over here one night recently, and listened to the sounds of Kate and Josh waking up in the next bedroom. They were laughing and giggling, and Josh was teasing his mum, saying, "You've got chooky hair" — saying she looked a bit like a chicken. They were having such a delightful time, and I felt my eyes fill with tears and got quite indignant with Andrew at that time, thinking to myself, "You should be here with Kate and Josh and Caleb in bed laughing about chooky hair."'

But Sara reflected that she and others had been amazed by Kate's approach to life since losing Andrew. 'Although people expected Kate to be completely demolished by her grief, she wasn't, because in the years she was married to Andrew they had a fantastic relationship. It wasn't the same relationship I have with my husband, but she knew they were giving each other everything they could, and she knew he was a vulnerable, sensitive person, and she was the right person for him. They worked really hard at everything, and there were no regrets.'

In the weeks that followed, Kate, as a single mother, experienced hard times. It was ten months now since Andrew had died, and there was still no sign of the coroner's inquest, which alone could finally lay the matter to rest as regards what had actually happened to him. Kate left messages with the coroner's office, but apparently to no avail.

In October floods swept through Kate's suburb, and the damage took weeks to clean up. A month later, a burglary — Kate's house was ransacked, her stuff strewn everywhere. But somehow she was able to tell Sara delightedly that the burglars had missed one special drawer in which she kept the things most valuable to her — wedding rings and other special memories of Andrew. But expecting her to press on with good grace was demanding a lot. There had been an amazing conversation with a new case worker, who'd taken over Kate's file at Income Support.

Kate related the conversation: 'This woman said, "I'd just like to know where this baby came from." I looked at her blankly. I guess I felt winded — I was out of breath when she first said it. She repeated, "I'd like to know where this baby came from?"' Kate was smiling as she was telling me this.

'I said to her, "Well, gosh, I was pregnant when my husband died." The case worker said, "Oh, sure you were!"'

Kate went on: 'I said, "Well, I was. You'd only have to do some calculations to work out I was pregnant." The woman asked me if I had a birth certificate for Caleb, and I told her I did — feeling quite proud that I did — and she said, "Well, consider yourself very lucky that you've got one, because women in similar situations have great difficulty obtaining them."'

Kate, still a little stunned, had taken Caleb and Josh down to Income Support with the birth certificate. In the end everything had been fine — the case worker had finally said she believed Caleb was Andrew's son. Throughout our interview on this matter, Kate kept smiling her cheeky smile. I thought to myself that she was incredibly gracious and felt again how valuable it was to have a sense of humour.

On 18 December 1998, one day short of a year after Andrew's death, the coroner's court ruled he had died at his own hand, re-marking that the balance of his mind had been affected and that he'd been under severe stress.

Kate doesn't believe what happened, as Andrew pressed on at Hutt Hospital, was anyone's fault in particular. She simply hopes the loss of her husband, and others whose state of mind leads them to take their own lives, will raise awareness of the sad and dark places depression can take people.

'I see depression more now as being like any other sickness, any other chronic illness. The big difference is, with things like diabetes, asthma and heart disease there isn't any shame that goes with them, but there still is with depression, and that's what Andrew died of — he died of depression.'

Andrew's passing undeniably brought Kate the worst pain she can imagine anyone going through, but her message is 'This is survivable'. And her faith certainly made a difference.

The coroner's verdict in, and a sense of closure settling, Kate stood with me at Port Nicholson, on the Wellington waterfront, and reflected on what she felt she'd learned in the past year.

'I know that God has an eternal plan, that He's given me some amazing days this year, amazing days of grace. He's stood next to me. What have I learned? Life's tough, but God's faithful.'

UPDATE

Kate Dominikovich has found herself in demand as a speaker and counsellor all over New Zealand. Her story, as told in the series *Extreme Close Up*, has been aired several times, and after every screening she has received calls from people who have either lost loved ones to suicide or attempted suicide themselves.

She remains as stroppy as ever. She won a place at a Tiger Woods golf clinic when the great man was here in early 2002. Minders told her not to bother trying to get Woods' signature on the picture of Josh and Caleb she'd brought with her, but after the clinic she broke through the cordon and held the picture just inside Woods' car as the door was about to close. The golfing star smiled and wrote a nice greeting for the boys.

Last Christmas, Josh — the ever-faithful child guardian of his mum and little brother — showed a streak of vulnerability. The children in his class were asked to choose what they'd especially like Santa to bring. Josh's project, now hanging in Kate's lounge, asks simply, 'I wish that my Dad would come back on Earth for Christmas.'

7

THE LONG WALK OF DAVID GREEN

I first met David Green at a Salvation Army conference in 1998. He was a resolute kind of fellow — wore the Sally uniform with pride and grabbed your hand with a firm grasp. But you had to lean down a bit for the handshake: David Green, insurance salesman and air-crash survivor, was in a wheelchair. I was so impressed with what he told the Army men's breakfast that morning I sought permission to relate his story on television. It was quite memorable.

On a terrible winter's day in 1995, an Ansett New Zealand plane en route from Auckland to Palmerston North was caught up in some extremely bad weather. To make matters worse, as the crew tried to bring the plane in to land, they struck a problem with the landing gear.

Before anybody appreciated how serious the problem was, the plane had crashed into the Tararua Range. The actions of the Dash 8 captain, Gary Sotheran, would later become the subject of a highly publicised prosecution, in which Sotheran was charged with manslaughter, a charge of which he was later acquitted.

The aircraft broke into several pieces on the rain-swept hillside. Three people, including a flight attendant, died at the scene; others, suffering a range of injuries from minor to serious, were airlifted to a nearby hospital. Passenger Reg Dixon had been badly burned and died after transfer to Wellington Hospital.

Among the more critically hurt was David Green. He'd suffered serious fractures to his back and lost almost all his blood. Four ribs had been fractured and both lungs punctured. Still deeply unconscious, David was airlifted to Auckland for further treatment and assessment. Mercifully, of those initial hours of injury and severe trauma he has only limited memories. But his life had been radically changed.

As we began our interviews with him, a few years after the crash, David reflected on the crucial decisions you make in your life that alter everything.

'It was going to be a week of fairly complex travel arrangements. I had business to do in Auckland and Palmerston, and I was going to try and fit in a night with my mum in Auckland in the middle of it all. But I was dithering a bit. Shall I, shan't I? So I looked in my diary and was reminded that I'd recently set some goals for myself. One of the key goals — to spend some more time with my mother. So I made the decision — and the outcome of that decision was that instead of flying directly back home to Wellington, in order to keep some appointments in Palmerston I found myself on that little plane.'

After a lengthy spell in intensive care, David was moved to the Otara Spinal Unit. It was one month since the crash. 'All of that time is quite a blur now,' David told me. 'I was doped up because of the pain, but I can remember them starting to break the bad news to me.'

The news was that his back was so badly hurt he'd probably spend the rest of his life in a wheelchair. David had a strong Christian faith, and he was a member of the Salvation Army, but even his belief in God didn't stop him grieving badly over the loss of personal mobility.

'I came up to the gymnasium at the spinal unit one day,' David recalled. 'I'm a tough guy, but I burst into tears when I saw the other people sitting around with their disabilities and suddenly realised that I was now a cripple too.'

David's rehabilitation was a painful affair. At one point he had to lie perfectly still on his back for more than a month so a bad pressure sore could heal. But slowly he figured out what he was capable of doing.

'One night I got very excited,' he remembered. 'I woke up to realise that I'd rolled over in bed by myself. Within a few weeks I was able to tie my own shoelaces. More progress than I'd thought possible.'

But that was about as far as David got. And getting his shoes on was, in one sense, a rather academic exercise, because his soles would not be getting a lot of wear. His back injury was apparently severe enough that he'd never be able to manage more than a couple of steps.

Over the years in reporting you meet plenty of people whose misfortunes turn them bitter, and in some cases of such serious injury you find those who start to question even whether they want to go on living. There was no sign of that in David Green. He gave every impression of wanting to seize his new existence by the throat and make it work for him. He decided to stay in Auckland for his rehabilitation. The sheer hard work involved in getting himself up every morning on his own in his little flat was huge. Never a word of complaint, however.

By this stage, fallout from the plane crash was starting to emerge in the legal area. With four dead and many injured, people were beginning to talk seriously about whose fault the crash may have been. David's life had been shattered, and there was a strong expectation that if anyone deserved major compensation it was him.

The system of accident compensation in New Zealand meant David's rehabilitation was fairly comprehensive, but a firm of American lawyers was approaching all of the survivors from the crash, offering them the chance to sue the manufacturers of several parts of the aircraft. The lawyers said they would contend in court that these parts had not performed properly during the crisis, leaving the manufacturers liable. One item was the ground proximity warning system, which, the lawyers would contend, did not sound till way too late for the pilots to take evasive action.

The San Francisco-based lawyers told David he would be the star witness in the case. Of those who had survived the crash, he was the most seriously hurt. 'Because I was in a wheelchair,' he said, 'they said I would be the most compelling witness in an American courtroom.'

The lawyers told him they fully expected the American companies being sued to want to settle out of court, and that if he was the 'visible face' of the intended court action, he alone could expect to be awarded at least US$5 million. But something very profound had happened to David Green in the process of contemplating the future.

To hear this man speak his heart for even a short time is to be aware he has strong personal convictions. One weekend while he was praying about his predicament, David said he had a very strong impression. 'It was as if God was saying, "I want you to forgive everybody involved in this crash,"' he recalled. 'There seemed to be another part to what God was saying to me. The message was so clear: "David, one day you're going to walk again."'

People found his consequent decision — to let the case go — difficult to comprehend. Many were urging him to take the money, even if he then gave it all away. But his mind was made up. 'If I attempt to get money out of people, that will be tantamount to me not forgiving them, and I don't think my heart will heal,' he told me.

I pondered David's words after that first interview: I was no stranger to the notion of divine healing, having spent many years in a church where prayer for the sick was a commonly accepted practice, sometimes with very favourable results. But I had recently been asking myself some quite deep questions about the process of praying for healing, like why there seemed to be more failures than successes, and what unanswered prayer might mean for the faith of the disappointed believer in the longer term.

Still, David Green was so ruthlessly determined to walk again the mixture of faith, willpower and optimism made a heady cocktail. He saw things very plainly:

'It's a matter of principle,' he told me. 'It's like the law of gravity; when you drop something — whether it's a feather or a brick, it gets to the ground. Forgiveness, I've learned, is also a principle, and whether someone has banged your car in the car park or your legs aren't working, it all comes back to the same principle of forgiveness — putting it behind you and getting on with life. The numbers might be different, but the principle is the same.'

When we began filming, David was undergoing intensive

physiotherapy. Five mornings a week, he'd leave his little flat and wheel himself round the corner to the Laura Ferguson gymnasium for the disabled. It was a beautifully appointed but sobering place to visit. Slow-moving young men with bland visages — car and motorcycle crash victims mostly — fighting the haze of brain injury, learning to connect mind and limb again.

It was like watching someone preparing for an alpine traverse. David would go through a lengthy series of stretches, then strap splints to his calves. He would then haul himself out of his wheelchair and take several tortured steps, supported by a pair of crutches. He looked like a wounded stick insect, savaged by a cat, trying to haul itself to safety.

The effort would leave David exhausted and flushed. But staff at the gym were not the least bit discouraging: quite the reverse.

'If he could manage a hundred steps a day, that would be the equivalent of perhaps getting around his house, doing a series of basic chores,' the physiotherapist, Suzie Mudge, told me that first day. By the time of our third visit to the gym, David was up to 93 steps, and proud of it.

His doctors were telling him not to expect a massive recovery, but that continuing to work out at the rehab gym would do no harm. Dr Richard Seaman, an expert on the spine, told me as we looked at David's x-rays one day:

'While I have always wanted to encourage his positive attitude, I have consistently tried to temper that, and tell David he has had a very severe injury to the lower part of his spine, and it may be that he won't fulfil his dream of striding around the place.'

I asked David's permission to hang around with him, with a camera, for a few weeks. He lived alone in his small flat — two marriages under his belt — but was so focused on his rehabilitation he always seemed occupied and happy. He struck me again and again as one of those rare creatures who would probably emerge with contagious good humour even if he were run over by a steamroller. Happy to fly once more, he wheeled himself in and out of airports quite regularly, going off to speaking engagements and conferences. Ansett New Zealand was treating him well — free travel wherever and whenever.

Happily sporting a tie decorated with a design of teddy-bears

111

with parachutes, David related how he'd get into amusing conversations with fellow air travellers. 'Inevitably, when I tell people how good the airline is to me, they ask why that is. "I'll tell you after we've landed," is my usual response. No sense in getting anyone uptight.'

While we were compiling our story, the pressure kept coming on David to join the legal action, but he continued to say no. I wanted to see something of his resolve at first hand. I love the power of 'for instance' in television, and more as a journalistic exercise than anything else we took David out in his wheelchair to see what US$5 million would buy.

We showed him one of the finest boats at the best marina in town — about US$3.5 million dollars' worth. We asked him to imagine himself up in the wheelhouse, taking the vessel for a spin up to the Bay of Islands. We looked at half-million dollar European cars — which even we had to admit were not paraplegic-friendly — and took him round some lovely real estate.

With a good-natured grin David shook his head at all of the temptations. 'Wheelchair ramps around this flash house would cost me way too much,' he laughed as I pushed him round the edge of a gorgeous pool at a home in St Heliers. I had to conclude he genuinely was quite content.

Finally I took David to lunch with some people who had become his friends since the accident. They were the local members of Christian Fellowship for the Disabled — folk with a range of mental and physical challenges, lovingly cared for by selfless volunteers in suburban Auckland. As we sat having lunch with these dear souls of such evidently limited means, I put something to him: 'Many people I've spoken to about your principles,' I said, 'have asked me, if you won't take the money for yourself, why don't you grab it for people like these?'

David was incredibly good-natured about our prodding. It was evident, too, that his thought processes were not those of a religious ascetic. He really believed he should put the crash and everything associated with it behind him. Looking round at his fellow disabled Christians at the lunch they'd put on for him, he told me he believed his principles concerning forgiveness were not bendable, no matter how worthy the cause.

What I most wanted to see, as a programme maker, was the San Francisco-based lawyer, Terry Ford, trying to convince David to change his mind. This would obviously be a defining moment in the story — legal persuasiveness meets uncompromising belief — and quite powerful, no matter which way the discussion went. Ideally, the meeting would take place when Terry came to New Zealand on a scheduled trip to advance the case. Both parties were receptive to the idea of us being present with a camera.

But this idea came seriously unstuck in a most bizarre way. In fact, when Terry rang to say he couldn't make it to Auckland for the discussion, I almost did two things: fall off my chair with amazement, and wonder whether he was telling the most outrageous porkie to wriggle out of the meeting.

'I'm calling from Austria,' he croaked down the phone line. 'And I'm sorry, I can't make it to Auckland to do that TV thing with you.' His voice had a somewhat manic edge to it, and the cynical journo in me wanted to verbally beat him up and call him a chicken. But what came next was in the 'too weird to be made up' category. It turned out Terry needed to get home to a most unusual family situation.

While he'd been in Europe on legal business, his daughter had been out for a spin in his brand-new Mercedes convertible. While cruising along the freeway near her home in San Francisco, the young woman had noticed frantic traffic action in her rear-vision mirror. A police pursuit was under way. She could see the fugitive vehicle weaving across the lanes with Highway Patrol in hot pursuit.

She tried to manoeuvre out of the way, but the fleeing driver headed at speed into the same lane a car or two behind her. The next few moments were a nightmarish blur for the girl, as the runaway vehicle crashed only metres behind her with a sickening crump. The errant driver was decapitated, and his head ended up on the back seat of the Merc, dealing a mortal blow to the upholstery and rendering Terry's poor daughter catatonic.

'I believe she's getting professional help,' Terry told me, 'and I have to go home now to sort things out. Among other things, I'm gonna have to sell that car. No one's going to want to drive it after all this, I can tell you.'

It was one of those awkward moments when, because you have those nasty journalistic callouses on your soul, you wonder whether some light-hearted quip might be appropriate. But I restrained myself, and told Terry gravely that I understood. We arranged that when Terry got back to America he and David would have a phone conference on the proposed legal action, and we'd video the thing on both sides of the Pacific.

The phone conference took place just before Christmas. With one camera set up in Terry's San Francisco office and another at David's home in Auckland, we recorded the US attorney's last pleas to David to join in the court case. It was a masterly performance at the American end, the gist of the argument being that David had a moral duty to his fellow passengers on the Ansett flight to be the potential star witness.

Down the phone line in Auckland we could hear the rustle of pages on Terry's desk. He wasn't opening a legal file: he was turning to a verse in the Bible.

Neat touch, I thought. Quote scripture to try to get underneath David's skin. 'You need to remember, David,' said Terry, 'greater love hath no man than this, than that he lay down his life for the brethren.'

David smiled a little on the other end of the phone. 'I understand that, Terry,' he said, kindly but firmly. 'But the Bible also says, "'Vengeance is mine,' says the Lord, 'and I will repay.'"'

Eleven thousand kilometres away Terry gave a slight smile in the direction of the camera we'd set up in his office, shrugged, and acknowledged he was up against principles and personal beliefs he wasn't going to be able to topple.

A couple of weeks later, I sat with David on the foreshore at Mission Bay. A neat, dapper figure, sitting contentedly in his wheelchair with a white hat, he watched a couple of his favourite people romping in the sand. His daughter Katherine and granddaughter Claudia had come up from Wellington for a visit.

'I'm able to handle all this better now,' said David as he drank in the sight of two fit and energetic people enjoying the beach. 'At first, this was a bit tough. On Labour Day 1995, I remember I had my first major outing after the crash. A good friend came and picked me up and brought me here. The shore was covered with people, out having fun, playing with their kids. I couldn't get out of the car, so we had a kind of a picnic there. Katherine was pregnant at the time, and it struck me then that when the time came, I wouldn't be able to run around on the sand with my grandkids. A lot of emotion that day.'

Now, several years later, it seemed David was a relatively content man. He slid down off his wheelchair onto a blanket on the grass, and talked with evident glee to Claudia as she raced back and forth. Maybe he was imagining the day when he might not actually rollick in the sand, but perhaps once again feel it between his toes.

'So what do you reckon?' I asked Katherine. 'Should Dad take the money or stick to his principles?'

Not much hesitation there from a very understanding daughter. 'Of course, I do worry about him — but if you tried to make him do stuff that cut across the grain of his beliefs, he wouldn't be happy, and he wouldn't be true to himself. I guess the only thing that concerns me is the thought that in his old age he could do with some extra financial assistance, but I'm not about to try to pressure him. It simply wouldn't be right.'

When David Green's story went to air, the reactions were fascinating. People collared me in the corridor at work for days afterwards, either to ask, 'Was that guy for real?' or to tell me to pass on to David how much they admired him. As the feedback came in over the next couple of weeks, it seemed the most support for the injured man's principles was to be found around factory smoko tables. Many people apparently felt David had put on a brave performance.

About two years later, I was at another Salvation Army function in Wellington. 'You need to go and see David,' said one man, pointing enthusiastically. I wandered over to David's table, fully expecting to see the familiar shape of his wheelchair below the tablecloth. But there was no such thing. David confidently got to his feet from an ordinary chair and leaned on two walking sticks.

He gave a broad grin, and I shook my head in amazement. 'I'm still not quite there yet,' he said. 'I'm still using the chair a fair bit, but don't you reckon I've made progress?'

What could I say? Here was a man who didn't have a bitter

bone in his body and who still fully believed a broken back was no obstacle to walking again.

The journalist in me always wanted to know from David whether, if he'd had a chance to wind back the clock and not take that flight in June 1995, he would have taken it. When I asked the question, I was reminded again what a steely resolve the man possessed.

'You know,' he said, 'I don't think I mind the fact that I was on that plane. Sounds strange to say that, doesn't it? But so many good things have happened to me since that day. I've met some wonderful people I never would have met otherwise. You don't get to be in a special community like the spinal unit unless you're forced to live there. Sure, I wouldn't volunteer to have the kind of injury I've had. But no — no regrets.'

UPDATE

When I spoke with David recently, he told me he only uses his wheelchair now when he goes out. The rest of the time, around the house and office, he manages with a pair of sticks. He's married again, and he and his wife, Jill, live in Wellington. By the end of 2002, he's hoping to be completely off accident compensation and working full time again as an insurance consultant.

David heard that the legal action against the American companies over allegedly defective aeroplane parts did not, in the end, succeed.

In 2001, the pilot of the Ansett plane, Gary Sotheran, was found not guilty of manslaughter in the High Court at Palmerston North.

8

THE GALLOPING GRANNY

They reckon a bad upbringing can predispose you to turning out pretty crazy. If that's even partly true, by the time she reached adulthood Judy Moore should have been in big trouble.

When Judy was about 12, her family fell apart and she hit the streets. She started living rough under bridges, begging a bed from friends, or anywhere she could get out of the cold. In her later teens, she came under the influence of some people who helped put her back on the straight and narrow, but the Christchurch kid never forgot how to be streetwise, and she never lost her heart for the underdog.

Judy's story, and how she had made a career of helping people, were to unfold for me during one of the most moving journeys I've ever made — to the Balkans, in the latter part of 2000. About a year earlier I'd sat down with some friends from the aid agency World Vision as they tried to figure out the best way to promote their fine work on television over the following 12 months. I had always thought these guys were worth helping — partly, I guess, because of a strong family connection. My sister-in-law, Heather, had spent years in the field for World Vision, working in places like Romanian orphanages and reuniting displaced children with their parents after the Rwandan genocide in 1994.

'Why don't tell some of your hero stories?' I ventured at the meeting. 'From what I understand, you've got some of the world's most creative and innovative people out there making a huge difference in the field, so why don't you let a documentary crew get under their skin and show a TV audience what makes these people tick?'

At the time I wasn't actually pitching for the work, but World Vision got so enthusiastic about the idea they asked me and my coproducer, Linda Gollan, to take on the challenge.

'Who are your hard cases, your real "number eight wire" people?' I asked. 'I want some hard-headed individuals. They don't have to have too many airs and graces — just people who epitomise the kind of sacrifice and guts it takes to go into these difficult places.'

Graham Sterne, from World Vision, grinned, and I could tell that among the people he had in mind there were probably going to be some ideal candidates for stories. 'How about the Galloping Granny?' he asked, with a twinkle in his eye. 'She's about five foot nothing, dresses in leathers; the last time anybody saw her she was in a customised Cadillac convertible. She's right in the thick of things on the border of Kosovo, and she doesn't suffer fools gladly.'

'Perfect!' I responded.

What an amazing project it turned out to be. I soon found myself with my camera in the highlands of East Timor, with a Kiwi logistics expert, helping World Vision bring rice to needy villagers. Not long after that, Linda headed for Mongolia, where Peter and Sue Bryan, from Nelson, worked with street kids in the capital, Ulan Bator, rescuing youngsters from the holes in the ground where they congregated round buried heating pipes for warmth and shelter. We were collecting some truly heroic stuff.

The last two stages of the doco were to be recorded in the Balkans. It was a dodgy trip from the outset. Linda and I were instructed to wait at Zurich airport for 'a tall man with sunglasses', who would bring us our tickets for the Montenegrin Airlines flight to Podgorica, the capital of the Yugoslav Republic of Montenegro. The tall guy with the sunglasses never showed, and I handed over copious quantities of Swiss francs to a man purporting to be the gate agent. Somehow we ended up on the plane — filled with fellows who had ominous looking bulges under their jackets.

During the flight, I delved into a folder of clippings. Montenegro, it seemed, was something of a potential powder keg just at the moment. The territory was still part of Yugoslavia, the larger part of which consisted of Serbia, where the besieged Yugoslav president, Slobodan Milosevic, was running out of options. But Montenegrins appeared to be on the brink of declaring themselves independent, and rumours were growing that Milosevic might soon use military force to bring them to heel. Montenegro provided his last route to the sea, and it was feared the same bloodshed that had wracked Croatia, Bosnia and Kosovo might soon be unleashed there.

My World Vision information pack told me Judy Moore, who'd worked in this region tirelessly during the Kosovo conflict, was about to end her posting as country director for Montenegro and move into a new role as an area programme manager in neighbouring Albania.

Our plan was to shoot the segment on Judy, then drive east from Montenegro into Kosovo to shoot another — a delightful story about a Kiwi actor called Aaron Ward, who was returning with us to give a reprise of his performance as a clown teaching refugees, through mime, how to avoid getting blown up by land mines. Interesting mental picture!

When so many of your impressions about the place have been shaped by the six o'clock news, you expect to find anywhere you travel in Yugoslavia somewhat dinged up. Podgorica airport did have a couple of the obligatory burned-out bits of military hardware lying next to the runway, but otherwise, on what was a gorgeous September evening, the region looked peaceful, if a little threadbare.

That evening we drove through what could have passed for a Tuscan landscape perhaps a generation earlier. It made sense almost immediately that Milosevic would desperately want to hang on to Montenegro. Linda, Aaron and I were made comfortable in great World Vision digs not far from the centre of town, and before we'd even had time to unpack, there she was, at the door.

Five foot nothing, indeed, and with a smile as wide as a barn door. Judy Moore might be small, but she radiated energy. She projected a friendly but no-nonsense persona that must have suited her well during the bitter winter months of 1999, when she'd pushed through mountain passes with convoys of food for desperate refugees from Kosovo.

'Gidday! Want a beer you guys?' she almost shouted through the doorway, and that was fairly much the down-to-earth level at which the next four days were conducted, with a woman who filled me with a huge feeling of admiration. Judy had stepped into an incredibly complex situation in the Balkans, and been bombarded daily with the illogical political realities of the troubled region, but she was resourcefulness personified.

The next day, she took us up through the mountains to the eastern part of Montenegro. She had tales of 18-hour days in the area the year before driving convoys through the snow to bring milk powder to women who'd given birth while on the run from the Serb forces in Kosovo. Perils, some of bizarre nature, were everywhere, she explained, as we drove through one of many tunnels bored through the mountains.

'Needed someone to go through each tunnel on icicle patrol,' she told me. 'Big icicles — some two metres long. They hung from the roof of the tunnel, and the rumbling of the truck could shake them loose. Not a good way to die — a big icicle spear through your chest. Hence the advance party.'

One of our first ports of call was a little eastern town called Berane, near the border with Kosovo. Although battered by war, the region was quite picturesque. The town stood beside a river flowing swiftly over rocks — reminiscent of the central North Island. Here Judy had found a huge and desperate need. 'Three hundred and sixty people, one toilet, one tap, and babies being born under cardboard boxes,' she recalled as she looked at an old community centre we were driving by.

Huddled in fear inside this building had been Roma — local gypsy folk, who in many ways came off worst out of the Kosovo difficulties. They were perceived as the enemy by both sides, and no matter where they wandered they were vilified and in serious danger. Realising the situation was going to become intolerable, Judy had driven round the Berane district frantically looking for vacant land. When she at last found a place, the local authorities were amenable, and Judy set about building a proper camp in which to resettle the Roma.

'Some of them had been living rough for weeks, even months,' she told me. 'Babies had been born under trees; people had marched through two-foot snow drifts just to find what passed for safety for a few days.'

On a balmy afternoon we were ushered into the camp Judy had built — a collection of near-new huts, each about the size of a New Zealand double garage.

'Not bad for twelve thousand bucks, eh?' Judy said with a beaming smile, slapping the wall of one of the houses. 'If you can get someone with a few dollars to spare in somewhere like America, hey presto, you've got housing for eight or nine people.'

Indeed, inside every house we found families for whom this was the swankiest accommodation they could imagine. Delicious-smelling stews were cooking on simple stoves, while in most homes a baby was being rocked in a makeshift cradle. Pausing at one door, Judy looked inside at the simple domestic scene and tears filled her eyes.

'This is why you do it — this is what makes it all worthwhile,' she said, wiping her face. Going a bit misty myself, I asked Judy to help me over the language barrier so we could speak to a man whose haunted eyes caught my attention.

'Can you ask him what his dreams are?' I ventured during the interview. Some translation, and then the answer came back very seriously. 'I think what he'd like to say to you,' said Judy, 'is that for the moment it's too risky for him to have any dreams at all. Simply to be safe for a while is his big dream.'

That did it for me. It was one of those rare occasions when I had to walk away to the edge of the scene and weep for a moment as I measured up the reality of this man's life against the incredible good fortune with which I was blessed as a well-off person living in safety and prosperity. I looked at the Roma kids playing with what few possessions they owned, and reflected that in my own household at that time our biggest decisions revolved around how many megabytes the next family computer would have.

There were to be many other such moments over the next few days, as Judy showed us some of the incredible work for which she had been responsible. One blisteringly hot afternoon we went to a place called Konick Camp, where there was an even larger settle-ment of Roma. As we came down the road, we were greeted by the sight of what looked like hundreds of car wrecks. The place seemed more a junk yard than a living compound.

'We shoved all these out of the way,' said Judy. 'It used to be a tip, but I realised its potential as soon as I saw it.' For a time, the refugees lived rough there, but at least they were under canvas. Judy's photos show row after row of big UNHCR tents.

'That first winter was rough,' Judy told me. 'The winds blew through here at about a hundred kilometres an hour, and all the tents went flying. You had eight hundred people wandering around in the snow, wondering what was going to happen next.'

There were big smiles from the camp occupants now, though, as Judy came by. They knew the face of their benefactor well.

It turned out that the indefatigable little woman from Christchurch had calmly ordered up hundreds of tons of scoria and turned the bulk of the rubbish tip into a well-drained and very tidy camp. Hundreds of families now lived in relative comfort, with fresh water, a medical clinic in which people were taught skills such as basic midwifery, and a basketball court.

Camped outside the wire perimeter, however, were dozens of Roma families in makeshift cardboard and metal shelters. This is where the hard choices arise: who gets into the camp, and who has to stay outside.

'I've been in the field for sixteen years,' said Judy as we walked, 'but I still cry lots of nights because I know that not all those people who are living out there under tin and cardboard can be accommodated here. There is a limit, but boy, it's hard.'

The next day Judy insisted we join her for a last look at the beauty of Montenegro before she left for her posting in Albania. With her driver, ominously named Dragon, she took us down to the sea, to beautiful little ports like Kotor, towns which used to be part of one of Eastern Europe's most popular tourist playgrounds, before the Balkans went mad.

On the journey, Judy proved she was a woman of a thousand and one stories. During the Nato bombing of Belgrade, she had been hauled in by the police for questioning. Eight hours of bullying, with no food and lots of aggro. At one stage she had tried asserting her rights. Eyeballing the big Serb interrogator she'd said, 'Hey, even in the movies, everyone gets a phone call! When do I get mine?'

The answer had been blunt and to the point: 'You have no rights! Now, shut up!' So she had, and had lived to tell the tale, along with lots of others.

After a swim that afternoon in the warm waters of the Adriatic, and a wine and pizza in an idyllic town square down on the coast, Judy asked Dragon to take us back to Podgorica. We hadn't been driving long when, on a steep and winding road, Dragon started to groan and slumped over the wheel. He managed to steer the Land Cruiser into a lay-by before stumbling out and collapsing by the side of the road. He hauled himself up enough to vomit violently, than lay back on the ground, still groaning. The rest of us looked anxiously at each other and tried to recall if we'd eaten the same kind of pizza as Dragon. It's amazing how quickly phantom stomach pains can arise at such a time.

'Got to get him to hospital,' said Judy urgently.

'Great. So who's driving?' I inquired.

Everyone, including the local guys, spent the next couple of moments whistling or examining their shoelaces.

'Looks like you are,' said Judy, flashing me a wicked grin, no doubt recalling how, on the outward journey, she'd told me the death toll on these roads was among the highest in Europe.

Brilliant. Twilight on a murderously winding mountain road, being honked and flashed by hoons in Mercs and BMWs probably flogged from Germany in insurance scams and on their way to pay dirt. Another of Judy's countless pieces of mesmerising information. Dragon lay next to me, Linda and Judy mopping his feverish brow. He sounded more and more as if he was about to expire. Even better. Dragon was going to cark it before we got to this nameless clinic they kept telling me to look out for.

I drove till it felt like we must be in Russia, but then sure enough, down a back road, there was the clinic. We hauled Dragon inside, into a room that looked as if it might once have been a casualty clearing station during the Crimean War. Judy bulldozed her way through the local protocol and prevailing apathy, and persuaded a nurse, as broad as she was tall, to put a drip in Dragon's arm.

A perfunctory examination and a quick verdict. Kidney stones. Common problem round here. Something about the water. But whatever was in the drip was starting to work, and Dragon was giving a bleary smile. I wondered if it was vodka. Judy joked with him, then told me in a loud whisper to film the floor. 'Over in the corner,' she said with a grin. What a sight. Discarded syringes and medical dressings, in the most unhygienic pile of garbage I'd ever seen. Would Dragon make it out alive, I wondered?

Out of nowhere, it seemed, Dragon's cousin arrived in a beaten-up car. He looked well able to keep an eye on our guy, so we took our leave, knowing we still had a long drive ahead. As we left the little clinic, Dragon was nodding off to sleep, and the next morning we were comforted to hear he was OK and resting up in preparation for surgery. We could only hope the operation would take place somewhere where the floor had at least been swept since the last bit of knife work.

'No worries,' said Judy at breakfast. 'He's tough, he'll survive.'

There ought to be signs honouring Judy Moore all round Montenegro. From what we saw, it appeared she had moved through this region during her time as World Vision director trying to make a difference wherever she could. In one town we came across the country's only proper recycling plant. Judy had twigged to the fact that gypsies love to collect scrap and resell it, so she had organised a recycling station where they could trade their piles of metal and cardboard.

In another town further down the coast, she'd supervised the building of greenhouses. Here, Kosovo Albanian refugees who the year before had been fleeing for their lives had found not only security but also sustainable employment.

Back in Podgorica, with one day to go before Judy's departure from the country, we sat on her balcony and conducted a long and leisurely interview. Long and leisurely because we stopped periodically to listen intently to the sound of distant gunfire across town. I was goggled-eyed, but Judy scarcely batted an eyelid. 'Local Mafia,' she told us matter-of-factly. 'It'll be over drugs or petrol, or something like that.'

In the interview I sought to get under the skin of this woman. As much as anything I wanted to find out what the kind of life she led costs a person.

Judy, it turned out, wondered about that too. She had often worried about how her own children would judge her devotion to aid work as they grew older. After all, she had made some profound choices, which must, she figured, have had an impact on her kids. But there had been good times for her family — times of revelation, especially for her son, Clint, who'd spent time with her in some fairly gruelling front-line situations.

'When I went to Cambodia, Clint — who was just sixteen — came with me. I spent three years there, and he was mature enough to do some work. He would accompany the foreign TV crews who visited some of the fairly dramatic places around the country where people were still suffering the aftereffects of war. On those occasions, he'd come back at the end of the day with the visitors, and when I asked him how he'd got on, he told me simply that he'd had a good day. Not much feedback at the time.'

Judy was delighted to be able to tell us about a letter she'd recently received from her son, now based in America.

'He said, "Mum, I want you to know that I now understand why you spent so much time overseas helping the poor people." He told me of an experience he'd had while in Cambodia that I didn't know about. He'd taken a film crew through a place called the Soldiers' Hospital, a place that was especially for people who'd been blown up by land mines. Clint said a man was brought into the hospital while he was there, with one leg completely blown off and the other one only hanging by a few bits of flesh.

'The man had had terrified eyes and had grabbed Clint by his arm as he was being stretchered by, saying "Help me, help me," and then a few moments later he'd died. Clint told me he'd felt so helpless, not able to do anything to help that dying man. He went on to assure me that he now understood what motivated me, because he could see that what I was doing was making a difference and that I *wasn't* acting helpless; rather I was prepared to roll my sleeves up and get involved. He then told me he was proud of me. That was incredibly moving for me to read — I only wish I'd known about it some years earlier.'

For all that, Judy told me wistfully, being in the field had undoubtedly had a cost attached to it, from a personal point of view. 'I've missed out on the birthdays, the engagements, the birth of my grandchildren. There are inevitably going to be regrets about that kind of thing.'

But here's where you come across Judy's finely focused dilemma. You ask her how she finds going back to New Zealand for visits, and whether she feels she could ever settle there again after her years in the field. She thinks for a moment, looking off into the hills in the distance.

'You know, I once tried it for a few months and found it the hardest thing. You'd go back and sit in a comfortable lounge in Auckland, and someone would complain that their tea wasn't hot enough. It was all I could do to hold my tongue and not start raving on about the people whose desperate situations I've encountered over the last few years. No, I don't think I ever could go home and settle — it would be too tough.'

'So you think they'll be carrying you off the field in a box to your final resting place?' I asked.

'Something like that,' said Judy. 'Yeah, it's quite likely I'll die on the job.'

'What do you tell people when they ask if what you do makes a difference?'

'I look 'em straight in the eye and tell them with absolute certainty that I *know* working in this field honestly does affect people's lives and outcomes. Maybe it sounds like a simple thing, but I can help inspire a humble cleaner on a pitiful wage to become a computer expert, for example. I've seen that happen. If that only ever happens in one life, then all the years in the field have been worth it. It's more than about meeting people's needs for food and clothing — it's about dignity and purpose.'

We saw this principle in action later on that day, when Judy took us to a large World Vision storehouse just outside Podgorica. Here we were met first by the mangiest looking dog I had ever seen. It leapt all over Judy and licked her energetically. 'This is my refugee dog,' she told me proudly. 'Got him for ten dollars in a camp; he was about to croak and almost got run over by one of the bulldozers, and I couldn't bear the thought of it, so now he lives here.'

'Here' was a large white building in which World Vision housed its emergency supplies, ready to be taken out to the field. A woman emerged from behind the doors of the storage facility. She was built like a front-row forward, and embraced Judy in what I felt

126

sure must be a bone-crushing hug.

'Here's a classic example of a life that keeps getting better in tough times,' Judy said. 'This woman's called Antonia — she was a refugee from Bosnia. She'd made a few dollars cutting hair from time to time but was in fact very desperate. Now World Vision has helped transform her into a person with real management expertise. She runs the warehouse here and — look at the size of her — woe betide anybody who wants to come here and try to pinch anything!'

As if to demonstrate the validity of Judy's warning, Antonia began moving a few cast iron stoves around the interior of the warehouse as if they were little more than empty cardboard boxes.

We were impressed. There were gales of laughter between the two women as they discussed the latest emergency evacuation plan for if things got nasty. Milosevic's armies in the north were starting to rattle their sabres and threaten the little republic of Montenegro. With her arm round her much larger friend, Judy told us they'd been on the verge of heading for the Albanian border on several occasions, and had arrangements in place that would see everybody out of their accommodation and workplaces and into World Vision vehicles within a couple of hours.

'We had a code word and we think we like it so much we're not going to change it,' Judy said with a big smile.

'What's that?' I asked.

'Well, if we have to move out quickly, the code phrase over the radio will simply be "I've got diarrhoea"! Do you like it? It actually does convey the idea that you've got to go quite quickly, doesn't it?'

The warehouse echoed with uproarious laughter — it seemed this was a joke that translated readily into Serbo-Croatian. A few moments later, as we were drinking iced tea on a small porch, Antonia's big eyes filled up with tears as she took her Kiwi friend's hand and informed us all sombrely, 'This woman is my mother now, don't you know?'

In the clear afternoon sun, this was a great scene. Judy did some more reflecting — on the fact that not all postings bring such idyllic afternoons and time for developing friendships.

'Rwanda was the worst,' she said. 'Things were so horrific there, so fresh, that it affected everybody you knew.' For a moment her eyes wandered off towards the horizon and the brown hills of Podgorica, which seemed worlds away from the lush hell that was Rwanda and its surrounding refugee camps. She had become suddenly serious, her habitual effusiveness quelled for the moment by the memory of one particular day that will be forever etched in her memory.

'It started off with me consoling my secretary in the office in Kigali first thing in the morning because her father, who'd been macheted to death during the genocide, had only been buried in a shallow grave. She and some others discovered that dogs had dug up his body and were gnawing on his bones. Strange as it sounds, you get used to counselling people about these kinds of things, and I was trying to calm her down, but then there was a new crisis. It turned out that my driver had been denounced quite forcefully that morning as someone who'd taken part in the massacres. Because he was a Hutu and looked short in stature, someone had yelled out in the street, "He killed my brother," and the police had thrown him in prison.

'So this is all before I'd even had my first go at morning tea. And it kept getting worse. Word came through that the wife and kids of one of my staff members had been travelling in a bus. A grenade had been thrown into the bus, killing everybody on board, so my next task was to find the staffer and inform him that his family had been wiped out. As if that wasn't enough, my administrator was quite desperate that day, because a couple of days earlier one of his neighbours had been murdered and thrown down a well. The neighbour's wife, as part of her punishment, had been thrown down the well too, and had had to lie there on top of her husband's body.

'When the hysterical woman finally made her way back out, she came to my administrator, her neighbour, pleading for help. He had to turn her away because if it was perceived that he supported her in any way his family could also be in danger. So he was a bit of a cot case still. So hey, welcome to Rwanda — just another day in paradise, I guess.'

For all this kind of drama, here was a woman who ate, slept and drank aid work, and had obviously learned to leap major hurdles in a single bound.

Judy's last day in Montenegro was at a staff retreat for World Vision workers — a day of fun, mostly, at a fairly basic outdoor restaurant on the outskirts of Podgorica. Once the new boss, an Australian called Ross Piper, had called everyone to order for the formal part of the day, I could see Judy shifting uncomfortably in her seat near the front. World Vision is businesslike and under-stated in the way it honours its heroes — there are, after all, a lot of them around the place.

After a brief tribute and the handing-over of flowers and gifts, Judy made a hurried exit. I was anxious: we needed that bit of visual closure for the story — the departure, the last hurrah. After a bit of searching, I found Judy had already headed for the big white Land Cruiser that was to take her to the Albanian border. She'd avoided the long goodbyes with the couple of dozen staff because she was weeping profusely.

'I never get used to this,' she sobbed. 'You put your heart and soul into places in the field, and leaving is always incredibly hard. It's like a baby you've given birth to. You've watched it grow, and then you have to hand the child over to someone else and just disappear.'

But composure came — along with a dose of typical Judy hu-mour. 'I was a bit horrified,' she said to me in a near whisper. 'I saw the first guy they said was going to drive me to the border, and I told them "No thanks!" in a big hurry. He's a bit dodgy, that one — threatened to kill me once — and I really need someone who likes me for this ride.'

The replacement driver turned out to be one she trusted, and without further fanfare she was off, heading for a new challenge, a new 'baby' to nurture.

UPDATE

'Tell me what you've been up to lately — I'm finishing up your chapter!' I e-mailed Judy recently. I could imagine her rolling her eyes, but she replied:

> I have been in Albania over a year now. This year I am build-ing four schools, and doing 'income generation' for people in

my region, with turkey and rabbit breeding. I've built three bridges so kids can go to school (they need to cross a river which floods in winter), I'm fixing a road so villagers can take their produce to market without it getting ruined, I'm putting down a complete water system for 200 families who have no water at the moment, and I'm building three health centres. I'm also helping about 30 village families build greenhouses and having them trained in water irrigation, composting, etc. so they can grow more veges to eat and sell; and putting up two electric transformers so villagers have a stronger electric current so they have lights to allow the kids to do their homework at night. There are a few other things, but those are the basics.

See ya, Judy

9

PLAYING WITH FIRE

Graeme Booth had what we used to call in radio journalism a
'magic' voice. Translation: one of those rare, gravelly voices that
carried authority and urgency when he read the news. 'Boothy', as
we called him, also had a penchant for fire engines. Many mornings, after he'd finished his early shift on Radio Hauraki, he'd be
off in a corner of the newsroom, a massive sandwich in one fist, a
phone in the other, talking earnestly, in that great voice of his,
about the red beasts that were the love of his life.

We'd smirk as he talked incomprehensibly to some joker called
Harry or Stan, down in Waiuku, about how they were going to
restore the old V8 low-pressure delivery engine from the Patumahoe
brigade, or something like that, in their spare time. At least that's
how I recall it many years later.

You see, Graeme was a volunteer firefighter. A rare breed. Nuts
about fire engines, and passionately devoted to a cause: that of
keeping his community safe.

This meant that while he worked in any newsroom — and I
worked with him in many over the years — the fire round was
pretty well roped off, and Graeme remained an object of fascination to the rest of us for his 25-year unpaid labour of love with the
Laingholm fire brigade. Sure, he copped his share of jibes about
being some kind of Oberführer for a bunch of Westie fire nuts, but
from Graeme there was always a good-natured grin, and a tale

about the latest drunk the Laingholm brigade had hauled up a cliff face, or a fire they'd dealt to — often saving someone's life in the process.

I mention all this to set the scene for the mind-bending story I covered in my first documentary of the new millennium — the strange business of firefighters who turned out to be fire-starters. Graeme came into work one day looking somewhat haggard.

'What's up, buddy?' I enquired.

He sat down next to me in the TVNZ café and shook his head slowly. 'Bloody cops,' he said. 'They've arrested a mate of mine, and it doesn't make any sense.' He then poured out a tale about one of the guys in his volunteer brigade. The fellow was called Keith Raymond. The police had picked him up the previous day and indicated they were going to charge him with a truckload of arson offences.

'It's crazy,' Graeme went on. 'Some of the fires they've charged him with — he physically couldn't have been there. It's nuts — Keith's got young kids, he's a dedicated member of the brigade. What am I gonna do?' He was clearly at his wits' end. As local brigade chief, he'd helped bring Keith onto the team, and he trusted the guy. Graeme's secure and tidy world was being shaken to its core.

He left our meeting that evening seemingly of the view that the police would ultimately realise they had made a ghastly mistake and drop all charges. But it was not to be. The case of Keith Raymond, businessman, volunteer firefighter and now accused arsonist, was destined to be an attention-grabber.

What made the subject especially interesting to me as a documentary-maker was that the case was just the latest in a rash of court hearings about fires lit by the very guys who were supposed to keep their communities safe from flames. Firebugs in the firehouse. So we set out to explore the phenomenon.

Keith Raymond had thus far made a very good job of avoiding the media. He was smart, all right. On one occasion, he entered a courthouse for a hearing wearing a suit and carrying a duffel bag. Having given the cameras the slip on the way in, he knew they'd be determined to catch him when he exited. But after his appearance before the judge, he slipped into the courtroom toilets, changed into completely different clothes, and departed without being noticed, leaving the puzzled media in his wake. So I was a little surprised when he agreed to see me, albeit without a camera to start with.

I met Keith at his business in West Auckland. He specialised in cleaning industrial clothing. The firm wasn't in great shape but he was still trading, and the trim, balding man in his late thirties looked about as far from being a dangerous firebug as it was possible to imagine.

'I'm expecting to go to jail,' he told me flatly, as we chatted in the office at the cleaning plant. 'It leaves my two little children without a father, my family without an income; their home will go, vehicles, everything. So to all intents and purposes it will destroy the family.' And from the sound of it, he was suggesting it was all the fault of someone other than himself.

'Did you light the fires?' I asked, straight out. A pause.

'Well, if I did, I don't remember. The cops hassled me into pleading guilty. There are some I've admitted to that I know I couldn't have been responsible for. Just too much pressure; I caved in to get the police off my back.'

Uh-huh. Interesting start, I thought. Time for some research on what had been going on out west.

Someone had been lighting fires in West Auckland for years. There had been hundreds of them during the mid to late 1990s — an apparently deliberate and malicious campaign. There had been five separate arsons at Rutherford High School — three million dollars worth of damage, ravaged classrooms, shell-shocked teachers and children. Principal Cliff Edmeades said the school had felt as if it was living under siege.

'It got into your head. All of us, kids and teachers, started thinking, "I go to a school where there's always fires!" Teachers were wondering, "Which block next? What do I have to duplicate? What should I be keeping at home? What should I be removing from the place? In the ordinary course of the day, what precautions should I take when I go home at night?" It was a terrible way to live.'

Then there were the deliberately lit fires at Piha Beach — scores of them — constantly tearing through bush and scrub, and threatening homes. Said residents like Margaret Byer: 'It was really scary, 'cos you'd go off to work in the morning and you wouldn't know if you'd have a house or even a community to come back to by the end of the day.'

One of the properties, hit twice by arson, was the lovingly tended estate of author and columnist Sandra Coney, a long-time resident of Piha. *Maggie's Garden Show* had only just finished featuring the rebuilding of the scorched property when the arsonist struck again. Onto the police inquiry came a cop with the determination to find out who was behind the fires. Detective Sergeant Gary Davy spent many hours listening to the heartfelt pleas of Piha residents, who wanted the arsonist caught.

'Sandra Coney and her family spent years and years and several thousand dollars to try to regenerate this bush,' Davy told me as we walked over still-blackened hillsides, 'only for it to happen again three-and-a-half years later. It was absolutely devastating for her.'

Davy showed me cliff-top homes where you could still see scorched vegetation nearby. Several homes had been just moments from complete destruction when frantic residents and firefighters had arrested the blaze.

The pattern at Piha had become deadly and scary. With nightmarish precision, the arsonist struck at two properties on the fourth anniversary of when previous fires had been lit. Bush, just recovering, was in flames again.

'They were too scared to go to work,' said Davy. 'They were too scared to go to sleep. They were just having fire after fire after fire, and they were extremely worried.'

I had to admit, even though I lived in West Auckland, the sheer scale of the problem had passed me by as a news event. Some residents must have felt someone was actually trying to kill them.

In desperation, one Piha resident, whose property had been torched more than a dozen times, put a video camera up a tree to see if he could record the arsonist at work. Every morning, he'd reset the tape and waited patiently for a result.

Switch scenes for a moment to another West Auckland community.

Laingholm is a small, bush-clad suburb on the upper reaches of Auckland's Manukau Harbour. The people there place a high value on community involvement. One strong weather vane of that community spirit is the local fire station.

Like scores of others around the country, it's run by volunteers — regular people, most of them with day jobs. Into their ranks, in 1996, came a man with a bit of a past — Keith Raymond. Not the easiest guy in the world to get on with, by all accounts — abrasive, and a problem person at his last volunteer base, the Te Atatu brigade. But Laingholm fire chief, Graeme Booth, asked his volunteers if they wanted to give Raymond another chance. Graeme had always been quite a compassionate soul.

'In Keith Raymond's case,' he told me, 'I saw the brigade before he was even offered a probationary period and told them this guy had had some problems at his previous station.'

However, there was a little more to the story. Keith had previously been under suspicion for starting fires, and Graeme says he told the Laingholm brigade about this.

'I said there's something else you all need to know: he has been questioned for arson. So I asked, "Do you want him in your brigade, or do I ring him tonight and tell him no?" and the Laingholm guys said, "We'll give him a try."'

Raymond wasn't universally liked at the little station, but he pulled his weight. Often he'd bring his small son along, sit him up on the appliance, and work for hours on end, cleaning and maintaining equipment, and building customised parts to improve storage on the fire engines. Was he keen to fight fires? Without a doubt. It would only be much later that his fellow brigade members would realise, with hindsight, that when he'd arrived for duty with an overheating engine, as he'd often done, he hadn't always simply raced in from home at high speed. Sometimes he'd been out lighting fires.

The Laingholm volunteers were as frustrated as anyone else in West Auckland about the spate of fires afflicting their neighbourhoods. In their own patch there had been dozens of blazes, at homes and on hillsides, that had all the hallmarks of arson.

On 18 February, at Piha, the camera up the tree struck the jackpot. It was a hot day — a likely day for the arsonist to strike, thought the cameraman. In fact, it brought better luck than the resident would have dreamed possible. The camera captured clear images of a vehicle coming up Piha Road. Then, a brazen act: an arm appears and something is deliberately thrown over the roof into the dry scrub.

Moments later a fire breaks out.

There are further images — of a car stopping and young men beating out the blaze with sweatshirts.

Police watched the video closely, again and again. The registration number of the car from which the object was thrown was unmistakable. The vehicle turned out to be owned by West Auckland businessman and volunteer fireman Keith Raymond.

Gary Davy and the West Auckland police moved in. 'The day before Raymond was arrested, we executed a search warrant at his address,' said Davy. 'His vehicle, the one in the video, was at his address, and a search of the vehicle found what I'd term an arson kit.'

Keith Raymond was arrested on 3 March. He would ultimately admit to starting 22 fires, dating back to 1994, although when first arrested he was charged with starting more than 50.

Among the fires Raymond admitted lighting were several that had caused significant damage to property, one that had injured a fellow firefighter, and many that had had the potential to kill. Needless to say, the arrest blew apart both the Laingholm brigade and the life of Keith Raymond's family.

'From my perspective, if I was to be charged with a crime, it couldn't be anything worse,' Keith told me in our first interview. We were sitting in the front room of his home; his wife, distressed and confused, had taken the kids out for a few hours. It was a sad little scene. A modest home, photos of the children in attractive frames, and, most prominently, a picture of Keith neatly attired in his fireman's uniform.

Keith appeared to be in a state of deep denial. Despite having pleaded guilty, he was rationalising what had happened, talking of police coercion, and raising the possibility that he might have been suffering from post-traumatic stress disorder when he lit the fires. Peculiar stuff was to come from his lips as we continued to compile our programme.

It had all come as a body blow to Graeme. I interviewed him in his office at the Laingholm fire station. 'I was utterly shattered,' he told me. 'It was like a member of my own family had been caught in something equally as horrible.' I had never really seen him emotional, but what this affair had done to him was unmistakable. Tears flowed as he looked round the station and pondered the fallout.

'It was bloody awful — just about tore me apart. I couldn't sleep. One of the worst times of my entire life. You know, you work so hard to build this little brigade up, and it was like someone had broken it. Everything that we stand for — preventing fires or extinguishing fires, or minimising the damage to property — it was shattered. If someone within our ranks had been responsible for those fires, it's the worst thing possible. You couldn't ask for anything worse happening.'

What was left for everyone to ponder were the huge questions about the man now facing trial for extremely serious crimes. Who was he really? Well, his employees at his cleaning plant didn't believe their boss was bad — he'd never given them any cause to suspect he was off lighting fires during the lunch break. And in the Laingholm brigade, although some had their suspicions, he was considered a very hard-working member of the team.

However, when you start to probe the Keith Raymond story, you find deep suspicion going back a number of years. In 1995, strange things were occurring at a place called the Auckland Institute of Studies — premises that had once been a maternity hospital and now specialised in running courses for foreign students. Someone was starting fires in various parts of the institute. It appeared the culprit was stalking the corridors, waiting for the right moment, then initiating mayhem.

Keith Raymond was employed as a cleaner there, and was also a volunteer fireman in the brigade at Te Atatu, some distance away. Fire prevention officers investigating the blazes suspected he was involved.

The Te Atatu brigade would not have been called on to fight the fires at the institute, which ruled out the idea of Keith seeking glory by riding in and receiving the credit for dousing the flames. But some of his activities as a cleaner seemed very suspicious. Among other things, he'd been found more than once on the end of a fire hose in a corridor, putting out a fire he said he'd discovered. Too many coincidences.

Fire investigator Grant Olsen told me: 'One thing you're always suspicious about is people who you consistently find at the scene of fires — whether they're volunteer firemen or not.'

Although charges were never laid, it all started to make sense to fire investigators and policemen once the videotape of the Piha Road fire was handed over. Even Graeme, who had wanted so badly to believe the police had got it wrong, said it was the unmistakable sight of the hand tossing the fire-starter out of Keith's car window that finally did it for him.

'Forgive me,' I said to Keith during our main interview, 'but it all looks pretty convincing.'

But he wasn't going to own up to anything. 'That vehicle,' he said, 'I don't own it for a start — it's a company vehicle. It's available to whoever needs to use it if I'm not around. Even members of the fire brigade have used it, to transport equipment for drills.'

In reality, however, the police had witnesses who'd seen Keith driving the vehicle at around the time of the fire. No credible excuse seemed possible. When I put his claim about the vehicle being available to others, including fellow members of the brigade, to Graeme, he just shook his head. It was almost like the last straw — a guy he'd once called a mate now desperately trying to raise suspicions about his former firefighter colleagues.

This man, whom the police were saying might be New Zealand's worst serial arsonist, had been so completely caught there really was no way out as his court appearance approached.

Curiously enough, although Keith denied he was an arsonist, he did leave open the possibility that he was a pyromaniac and didn't know it, his explanation for this being that he was suffering post-traumatic stress from his time with the Te Atatu brigade.

He cited a fire he'd attended at a house in Te Atatu — about 10 years earlier, he thought. He said he'd been crawling along the floor through thick smoke. His torch wasn't working. Stumbling, blind, into a room where he thought some children might have been, he felt around to get his bearings. It was stifling hot, and pitch black. He grabbed something that felt smooth but he couldn't see.

A fellow officer, coming in behind him, had a working torch.

'He flipped his torch on, and then I could see I was actually holding onto the leg bone of one of the victims. That's what the smooth object was, the leg bone of a young boy who had been badly burned and was now dead. On the other side, when the light went on, I discovered I was touching the body of a young girl who had mistakenly opened the wardrobe door, I would say, trying to escape, and had fallen into the wardrobe and died there.'

'I couldn't move. I just sat there, holding on to this kid's leg. It was quite a while. I went outside and I can remember walking down the driveway and taking my helmet off, taking my breathing apparatus set off and throwing it on the ground. I sat on the kerb in front of the fire truck with my helmet in front of me for a long time.'

Keith's view on all this now? It had affected him more than anything he could remember. The link between that occasion and the arsons 10 years later? His only concession was that he might have been angry and disturbed enough by what had happened that night to have snapped, and to have started, in moments he could not now recall, to become a very disturbed man who lit fires.

The police didn't buy this, and neither did Keith's own stress counsellor, Dr John McEwan, who told me, 'I don't believe a post-traumatic stress reaction creates arsonists. In this situation, if we have other factors, and he's angry and enraged at equipment failure, or the Fire Service, he may light fires to try to force the service to do something. Or perhaps he's driven by some other twisted logic. But it's not a post-traumatic stress reaction.'

Detective Sergeant Davy was equally unimpressed: 'I don't accept "blackouts" as an excuse. The premeditation involved in purchasing the items for the arsons — you know, the incendiary devices we found — and the fact that he was storing this stuff in his vehicle — that level of planning just goes to show that it wasn't a spur of the moment thing which just happened and he forgot it.'

But an enigma remained. Arsonists usually fit relatively straight-forward profiles: some get a sexual thrill from lighting fires, others have readily identifiable mental disorders. The most obvious category for Keith Raymond was the would-be hero or thrill-seeker. But Graeme said that didn't quite tally.

'Firefighter arsonists tend to want to ride to the fire on the fire engine, to leap out and be the big hero. Now, considering where these fires were lit, you have to understand West Auckland's a big area — lots of brigades. Very few of the fires Keith's supposed to have lit were in our patch. OK, sometimes we were asked to come in as a back-up, but even when we got there most of the work had been done — no great frontline work for Keith. So that part doesn't make sense.'

As Keith's court appearance approached, this very unusual man was flipping back and forth between proceeding with his guilty plea on the arson charges and going before a jury. The court and Keith's own lawyer, Steve Cullen, were getting frustrated. Cullen found his client's behaviour, motivation and mental state hard to fit into any known legal or criminal pigeonholes. I put it to him, 'Your client's a man with his own relatively successful business, an apparently stable marriage, two kids, and a fulfilling job in the community as a volunteer fireman. Why go and light fires?'

Cullen nodded. 'Absolutely. It's bizarre. That's why I said at the sentencing process that the Crown was in a difficult position when it tried to assert he was mentally normal. It was left in that quandary: he fitted all those criteria you've just been through, and yet if you accept the pleas he presented to the court, he was manifestly committing abnormal acts.'

In the end, Cullen managed to persuade Keith to stay with his original plea of guilty. In the week leading up to sentencing, I spent time with Keith at the factory as he started to put his affairs in order. There was such a sense of normality, which belied the awful truth. My eyes were drawn to his kids' colourful drawings on the wall of his office, just like I had at my work.

There was no logic at all. So much to lose: a brigade to which he was devoted, a business he'd worked hard to build up, a family he professed to love deeply.

'I don't think either of my children knows what's happening. I haven't told them. If they find out, if the time comes, I will certainly sit down and explain it to them. What is probably upsetting to them is the fact that all of a sudden when the Laingholm fire siren goes these days, Daddy doesn't get up and run out.'

As we waited for what would be the logical end point for our story — the final outcome of Keith Raymond's court case — we turned our mind to the broader picture. How incomprehensible this whole business was.

Volunteer firefighters are, by and large, an incredibly dedicated breed. They typically give up hundreds of hours of their time each year. The entrance exam is gruelling, and the job is hot, gritty, risky work, with no reward save the satisfaction of serving the community and the camaraderie that goes with this kind of activity. How could their ranks be infiltrated by loose units like Keith Raymond?

Here was the sting: Keith Raymond was one of 13 New Zealand volunteer firefighters to be charged with arson in a three-year period.

It was a mind-bending problem for the police and Fire Service. In Taumarunui, the siege mentality that set in when a season of arson began in the late 1990s was palpable. Someone was sneaking around at night lighting fires all over the town. Small stuff, a lot of it — skips and the like — but every now and then there was a big one. Like a classroom block at a local school.

Taumarunui's fire chief, in an all-volunteer brigade, was Barry Fisher. He took to doing personal patrols of the town on his way home from functions late at night. He drove us through the streets one evening, recounting his fearful sorties.

'I would just go all around on the way home, whatever hour it was, because I consider this town to be my town. In a funny way I felt it was my responsibility if fires were breaking out here, and I was getting really concerned.'

He had his reasons: somewhere, early in the piece, he started seriously to suspect members of his own volunteer corps might be responsible for the fires. 'I really worried about what might ultimately happen if it was any of my guys. There was a lot of feeling from the townsfolk at the time. It was starting to get out of hand.'

The police, too, were desperate to catch the fire-lighters. One officer hid in a large cardboard box by the side of the road, watching a prime spot in the heart of town. Sure enough, the arsonists struck there that very evening, but both the policeman and Fisher missed seeing the fire start; and in a cruel irony, Fisher, having been out on the streets that night, found himself under suspicion.

'The police had surveillance cover on it,' said Fisher, 'but never actually saw the incident happen. I had only just been past the scene when the siren went. So there was a fire where I had been only ten minutes beforehand, and naturally I was a suspect.'

After some close questioning, Fisher was told he wasn't seriously suspected of having started that or any other fire. But the authorities were no closer to finding the real culprits.

Some arson can be made to sound pretty harmless — boys with matches setting fires in rubbish bins, as was sometimes the case in Taumarunui. But in a close-knit community where more serious arsonists keep raising the calibre of their targets, real paranoia sets in. And sadness, too. We stood in a lovely little clearing with our camera one summer morning, at a spot above the town, and realised some arson destroys dreams that are never going to be rebuilt.

We were where the scout den had been. Hundreds of kids had come there over the years — it must have been the focus of countless happy memories. Now the Taumarunui aronsists had destroyed it, and there was no thought, in the prevailing climate of fear, of replacing it.

As fire chief Barry Fisher picked through the debris of these fires he was in a nightmarish situation. He really knew that guys in his own brigade were the likely culprits, but he couldn't prove it. And between suspicion and resolution lay the strong possibility that somewhere along the line someone was going to get killed.

Eventually, a lucky break in the investigations: three young men, all brigade volunteers, were arrested and the fires stopped. Huge relief for the town, but for Barry Fisher, as for Graeme Booth, a massive sense of betrayal upon learning that men he'd trained to fight fires were out actually starting them, just for the kicks they got when they then donned their uniforms and joined their colleagues on the engines racing to the scene of their crimes.

Fisher shook his head as he recalled the arrests. 'When it happened, quite frankly, I could hardly talk to anyone for two or three weeks without becoming emotional. It was almost as if there'd been a funeral, and the rest of the brigade at that time felt that way.'

It was one thing for us, as programme-makers, to tell the stories of small communities marred by firefighter arsons; in its own way that was quite easy. The harder part was trying to figure out the psyche of the arsonists, and how they had infiltrated the ranks of the brigades in the first place. The Fire Service was actually working quite hard, we found, putting measures in place designed to identify potential troublemakers right at the stage when they were applying for membership of a local fire brigade. It turned out the problem was actually a worldwide one, and the Fire Service was consulting an Australian expert on the matter, Rebekah Doley. She'd made several visits to New Zealand to help the service set up a system to assist guys like Barry Fisher and Graeme Booth spot arsonists before they wrought their havoc. But we'd found Keith Raymond to be so weird and impenetrable, we wondered how you could devise a foolproof system.

One of the young men jailed for his role in the Taumarunui arsons agreed to talk with us if we didn't show his face. He'd had a relatively easy ride, spending the last part of his sentence at home with a home-detention monitor on his ankle. We talked to him on the day a burly security guard took the monitor off, leaving him free to fully rejoin society. Prison and detention completed, and now in a full-time job away from Taumarunui, this former fire-fighter blamed too much booze and bravado for his arsonist exploits. But there was a sting in the tail of his remarks: he says that cocktail was dished up at the fire station.

'I was living in the fire station in some single guys' accommodation that was actually on site,' he told me, as we walked round the large property where he was now living. 'The environment in the station house isn't suitable for young people. They've got a bar there, and the alcohol is significantly cheaper than you could buy in a pub. You've also got no worries about ID, and at the time I joined the fire service I was only seventeen.'

The outcome, said this young man: a few of us drank too much, we egged each other on and we lit fires for a lark. It was a story that got a rather derisory response at the Taumarunui station house. As we filmed there on training night, the majority seemed well able to moderate their drinking and stay focused on putting out fires. When we turned up in late January, the bar hadn't been open since Christmas. The men and women around the station were like the bulk of volunteers we met at a dozen or so other stations around New Zealand: absolutely dedicated. Any thought of fire-bug mischief-making was light years from their minds.

I asked Fisher that night: 'Do you feel any responsibility as brigade commander that those young guys may have been to functions, got a bit liquored up and got out of control?'

'No, that's not the case, because a lot of these fires happened outside normal brigade hours.' In other words, it wasn't simply a matter of drink and daring and fires all on the one night.

Hearing allegations that it was 'all the brigade's fault' really made the other guys just plain angry. One Taumarunui volunteer, Naomi, was trying to raise two young children while training as a firefighter. She wondered what was the point of sacrifices like this if you were just going to blow it all by starting fires.

'They don't understand the danger they're putting people's lives in. Think about us guys going into a factory, for example. It's not as if it's just an empty building; we go in there, and we're on the line; there could be chemicals, anything. That's crazy.'

There was no single, logical thread to this rash of fires in the previous couple of years. The majority appeared to have in common only some twisted desire to relieve boredom or gain recognition. The hard part was that this aberrant behaviour was set against some of the finest traditions of selfless service we have in New Zealand.

Our 11,000 volunteer firefighters fight 40 per cent of fires, including more than two-thirds of fires in rural areas, and attend more than half of all motor-vehicle accidents. All out of community spirit. Auckland's fire chief, Paul McGill, told us, in an interview which I guess was supposed to be reassuring, 'It's a reality that we've got to face that a very small proportion of our people do want to light fires, and we know the profiles of potential problem people now. It's a need to be accepted. Often people who don't cope well in a social environment join the Fire Service, and maybe for the first time in their life they're accepted as part of a group that is doing good things for the community, and I guess by *lighting* fires they have that experience more often.'

How to figure out which firefighters are likely to be quietly making up a little arson kit in the back of their car? That's only part of the problem.

Whatever the Fire Service does by way of adopting a more restrictive vetting programme for recruits, in some parts of the country it's up against some unavoidable realities — mostly to do with a lack of willing, available people. In short, the spirit of volunteerism is not as strong as it once was. A senior fireman in Taupo spelled it out for us: 'In the old days we had a waiting list of people who wanted to join the brigade, and there was a three-month probationary period after which the brigade had a meeting, where all the officers spoke on whether or not you were suitable for the job. And everyone had a vote, and you had to have a majority or you didn't start.'

Another Taupo firefighter told me: 'Yeah, it seems to be a sign of the times. You don't get too many people wanting to volunteer to do anything these days, and so anybody who's got two arms and two legs basically they'll take on.'

Still, sometimes it seems a crisis, like an arsonist in the ranks of the local brigade, can galvanise a community and make people realise there's a job worth putting their hand up for.

Typical is the little North Island settlement of Mangakino, which was rocked in the late 1990s by the dreadful discovery that both the local fire chief and his deputy were deliberately lighting fires. People could scarcely believe the truth when it came out: fire chief Phil Chadderton had tried to create more work for his fire appliances in the mistaken belief he was about to lose one of them. Determined to finish our story on a positive note, we made the town our last port of call.

There's no doubt the Chadderton affair rocked Mangakino to its core; numbers in the volunteer brigade sank to unsustainably low levels, and mistrust ran rife in the community. A crusty former volunteer, Snow Westbrooke, summed up the parlous state of affairs after the boss had been sprung and carted off to court: 'There were only six members at the Mangakino brigade who were active, and three of them came and said we'd rather take some leave than get tied up in this arson thing.'

Snow was asked to take over the local brigade, leaderless and demoralised, and see if he could salvage something. So he and his wife, Joy, postponed the holiday they'd been planning for years, parked their house-bus out the back of the Mangakino station and gave it a go, shrugging off the hurtful remarks.

'You had to have a pretty thick skin at the height of it,' Snow told me over a cuppa in the house-bus. 'We were riding up the road on the fire engine in the Christmas parade, and things were said like, "Oh, there's the new chief of the arsonists." You had to grit your teeth a bit and be determined things were going to change.'

From the respect shown Snow around the station that afternoon, it was clear he'd done a good job, telling the few remaining volunteers to ignore the jibes and get on with their job of re-establishing credibility in the town. He'd obtained professional counselling for them, which had helped them channel their anger into rebuilding the brigade.

The results had been brilliant. Morale was now sky-high in Mangakino, and there was a full complement of 18 firefighters, with others waiting to join up. Snow had encouraged local youngsters to become involved, and had a big crew of keen, school-age cadets helping the adult volunteers take fire safety messages onto the streets. We watched some of them battle to hold a bucking fire hose in a drill at the station, as Snow shouted a few well-chosen words of encouragement.

No one was really any the wiser as to how the former fire chief could have deluded himself, and seduced others, into committing pointless acts of arson. 'There's no figuring that one out,' Snow told us; it was enough, he reckoned, that the townspeople trusted their firemen again.

'Once they got to understand that, hey, these guys aren't here to set fire to things, that there's no more "fires by appointment" in Mangakino, it all started to come right.'

And so it proved in every station house we went to where there had been a firebug in the ranks. New determination, new safeguards, more vigilance.

Inevitably, however, this arson business has resulted in a certain loss of innocence in some communities. Rutherford High School, where the spate of West Auckland fires began, used to have quite an open feeling. Now, everywhere, there are bars and barriers. Principal Edmeades just shrugged as he walked me past all the security measures. 'No choice now,' he told me; the school never wanted to live through something like that ever again.

Was Keith Raymond responsible for all those arsons? He still carries his secrets in a fairly murky mind, I've decided.

But what of him in the end? Well, the last time we saw him he was heading, on his own, for his date with the judge at Henderson District Court. All he was carrying was a thick paperback book. Still managing a smile.

'What are you reading?' I asked as we filmed him outside the court.

'Ah, *Kingdom of Shadows*. It's a good long read, and I think I'm going to need it.'

As he wandered into court, there was no sign of any accompanying family members. Although Keith assured me his wife believed every word of his protestations of innocence, we had doubts. She'd apparently been a very long-suffering woman, and word was the marriage probably wouldn't last his sentence.

Gary Davy, from the West Auckland police, was worried as Keith entered the court that morning. 'This offender doesn't show any remorse or take any responsibility for his actions. Unless he gets some serious help, no matter how long they lock him up for, I believe there will be a high danger of reoffending when he gets out.'

For fire chief Graeme Booth, at the Laingholm fire station, it was all the more puzzling, of course, because Keith was such a series of human contradictions. On the fire engine, Graeme showed us the ingenious devices and pieces of panelling Keith had installed during the many hours he'd spent there as a volunteer.

'This was all made by a guy who ultimately ends up going to jail for arson?' I asked, as we wrapped up the shoot.

'Yeah, that's right,' said Graeme. 'Can't get your mind round it, can you? It's just amazing. I've had guys from other brigades come here, looking at this appliance, and they ask, "Who did the work? Would he do it for us?" I say, "Well, there's a difficulty..."'

'When he gets out of jail?' I suggested.

'Yes, maybe when he gets out. Meantime, the prison service has fire brigades — perhaps he'll end up running that for them. Wouldn't put it past him!'

By the time the police van left Henderson District Court, Keith Raymond had been sentenced to five years in jail. His house was put on the market and his business went into receivership.

The Laingholm fire brigade got on with rebuilding belief in itself, and trying, like Mangakino and the other townships, to attract new recruits.

The volunteer corps of New Zealand firefighters had taken some heavy body blows during those years. But everywhere we went to cover the story, in every station house we visited, there was the same unquenchable spirit and the same firm conviction: the tradition of dedicated voluntary service would survive the heartache caused by a few.

UPDATE

As I finished writing this chapter, Keith Raymond was still serving out his sentence at Paremoremo Prison. He's expected to be considered for parole in 2002. Graeme Booth says Keith kept up a correspondence with him from jail, until Graeme wrote asking him to explain the incriminating video footage taken from the tree on Piha Road. At that point, says Graeme, the correspondence ceased.

10

NEW YORK, NEW YORK

The sound of the phone jarred me awake just before three in the morning. My wife, Ali, managed to pick up the receiver after several fumbling attempts and grunt into the mouthpiece. Initially her voice was a mixture of good-natured sarcasm and mild annoyance, as, I realised, it was her sister, Heather, on the line from somewhere far away. Heather is Head of Child Protection for World Vision in Washington, D.C., and she was calling to tell Ali she was OK.

'I'm so thrilled you're OK,' Ali offered sleepily, with a singular lack of enthusiasm. A pause. 'And why should I be glad that you're OK in Vienna?'

A much longer pause, and then, even in the dark, I sensed Ali's face going deathly pale. All she could muster next was a series of long drawn-out gasps, followed by a swift kick to make sure I was awake and a barked instruction to race upstairs and turn on the TV. It was the early hours of 12 September in Auckland — just before 11.00 a.m. on the 11th on the east coast of the United States, where all hell had broken loose.

I felt my heart rise to somewhere in the vicinity of the back of my throat as those images of planes hitting the World Trade Center were replayed again and again, followed by the sight of first one tower, then the next, collapsing into rubble.

Do journalists have a greater sense of unfolding history than

149

other people? Perhaps it's that the synapses in a reporter's brain start firing in a million different directions in an attempt to gauge whether a crisis is the beginning of the end of the world, and what his or her journalistic role in it might be.

Can any of us forget what that first morning was like, as we called loved ones, huddled round television sets, shook our heads and stammered out our astonishment to each other?

At the TVNZ complex, we were not only providing wall-to-wall coverage of what was going on, but also contemplating how we might put reporters on the ground near where the terrorist attacks had occurred. Within a couple of hours I had written a proposal to take a crew to New York to document what had occurred, and what might happen next in that great city, following the destruction of the twin towers.

Soon we realised there was going to be no getting out of New Zealand and into America in a hurry. Not only were no planes flying, but also the attacks had created such a backlog of air traffic that the chances of getting from Auckland to the west coast of the United States and then on to New York were very slim indeed.

Thirty-six hours rolled by, and we'd come to the conclusion the only way to get to New York without further delay was to fly the other way. Still with nothing entering American air space, we arranged flights via Hong Kong and London to Toronto, from where we planned to drive across the Canadian border down to New York. Sounds easy when you say it quickly.

In the event, by the time we arrived in London, American air space had begun to reopen and we changed our plans, climbing aboard one of United Airlines' first Boeing 767s to make the journey back across the Atlantic.

Heathrow Airport was a nightmare. For more than four hours we stood in queues being checked over, sniffed over and eyed up suspiciously because we'd changed flights, before being placed aboard a remarkably empty plane. The flight attendants all looked as if they were on heavy doses of Prozac, forcing what passed for smiles as they seated us for the journey. The captain's voice sounded incredibly flat as it came over the intercom.

'Good morning, ladies and gentlemen. I understand for many of you this will be the first time you have flown since the events of

September eleventh. The same goes for us. And as you'll probably be aware, many of us at United are still grieving deeply over lost colleagues. I want to assure you that our journey over to New York today is going to be as safe as we can possibly make it, and I want to enlist your cooperation.

'This is not the sort of thing you normally hear from your captain, but let me advise you that aboard this flight today we have a zero tolerance policy for any remark that is out of order, and I'm sure you know what I'm talking about. I would urgently seek your cooperation with this guideline, or else you may find yourself spending the rest of the day in a room with some people you don't want to know. Thank you and enjoy your flight.'

A kind of bemused glumness settled throughout the plane as we headed into a beautiful sky and began what I guess for everyone on board was an individual searching of the soul over what it must have been like for those who had sat in a rollicking 767 ride to eternity over New York, Washington or Pennsylvania only a few days earlier. I found myself full of deeply morbid thoughts, like how long does it take to die when a plane hits a building at 800 kilometres an hour?

I'd been to America more than two dozen times before, but what a strange feeling it was this time as we descended on a perfectly smooth glide path over the lower half of Long Island for the final approach into JFK. It was a gorgeously clear late-summer day, and below us we could see dozens of pleasure craft cutting up a wake in the blue water.

This seemed bizarre, almost irreverent. What were those people down there thinking? Going out and having fun only five days after such a terrible thing had happened on Manhattan Island? But the more I thought about it, and the closer we got to the smoky pall drifting off Manhattan out into the suburbs, the more *I* felt at fault — like an intruder, almost, at someone's funeral.

We hit the sack in our hotel near the airport, dog tired after more than 43 hours of travel, and drifted off to sleep to the sound of a Greek family celebration going on in the courtyard below us. In reality, the boats in Long Island Sound and the Greeks breaking glasses and plates below us were potent expressions of a people's determination not to be cowed.

The next morning, Monday, it was six days since the terrorist attacks. In the powerful final scene of Ron Howard's movie *Backdraft*, two fire engines from a Chicago station head into the sunrise to fight a major blaze in the city. The light was the same on the freeway as director Brett Cammell, cameraman Vaughan Scott and I edged towards Manhattan in the early rush hour.

This was the day when New Yorkers had apparently agreed with each other, unofficially, they'd go back to work in earnest and shake a fist at whoever had done this ghastly thing to their city. Fire engines were still streaming into the city from upstate New York to take over from firemen lost in the awful collapse of the twin towers. Several passed us, and other drivers waved flags and hooted and hollered, letting the firemen know the heroism of their mates had touched the hearts of every New Yorker, not to mention of people all over the country and round the world.

Initially, the closest we could get by vehicle to the site of the World Trade Center was about 15 blocks away, on a road called Canal Street. In the distance, across the police barricades, we could see a huge smoky haze rising from the scene of the disaster. This was only my fourth visit to New York, but I was sufficiently familiar with this part of the city to stand and gasp at the huge expanse of sky now visible where the towers had once stood.

Workers from New York's financial district, many wearing breathing filters over their faces, produced their IDs before a phalanx of cops, National Guardsmen and soldiers who were deciding who'd get into work and who'd have to stay away. Every now and then a distressed New Yorker towing a wheeled suitcase was turned back and told it wasn't yet safe to return home, down in the apartment complexes near Wall Street.

All along Canal Street we saw the first signs of the hundreds of makeshift shrines we were to see all over New York in the next few days. Wherever there was space, people had posted sheets and flyers showing the faces of missing relatives and detailing every feature, including moles and scars, that might be used to identify the body of someone who had not come home on the night of 11 September.

Wherever there were photos, there were also candles — many of them by now vast puddles of wax spilling across the footpath among wilting flowers, beautifully written poems, thank you letters to emergency workers, and, every now and then, a torn or defaced picture of Osama Bin Laden.

Every block or so, a lone protester with a poster of photographs and scrawl called for unspeakable things to be done to Bin Laden and his ilk. But the main impression that first morning was of the large, stoical population of the financial district resignedly making its way to work the best way it knew how, with the kind of head-down determination that characterises Manhattan Island. There was pragmatism, too: Ed Kaveney, a stockbroker on his first day back at work, spoke of a new spirit of 'noncomplaint'.

'There's no way round it now,' he said with a shrug. 'If they need to pat me down every time I go into my building from now on, to be sure I'm not a bomber, well, so be it. And if it has to be that way when I take my kids to a ball game, maybe it's the price we have to pay for enjoying our way of life.'

As Brett and Vaughan took pictures that morning, I found myself staring down one of the main avenues towards the scene of destruction, now so close I could taste the dust from it at the back of my throat and smell its fearsome odours. Right at that moment I experienced something that would trouble me a lot over the next five days: a peculiar numbness, the refusal of my emotions to allow me to get to grips with what had happened.

Why was this? After all, you'd think that, having been dropped slap-bang in the middle of the aftermath of perhaps the most awesome act of terrorism imaginable, I would be seriously choked up. A flood of possible explanations washed through my mind over the next few hours. Perhaps it was the sheer scale of the event, the notion that it was going to be harder to grieve for several thousand strangers than for any single individual to whom I'd been close. This might sound trite, but the more I thought about it, the more I suspected it was true. What had happened was way too huge to process in the way one normally dealt with grief or shock.

Maybe also I'd got tough over the years, and developed coping mechanisms to help me through situations of extreme trauma and even horror. My mind went back to a scene I'd encountered in a South Auckland house a couple of years earlier, where a young woman had been beaten to death by members of her extended family so they could steal her sickness benefit. I remember on that occasion being quite shocked with myself because I walked out of the house feeling virtually nothing — and being quite worried about it.

Analysing my reactions to that incident and how I was feeling now, I could only conclude that during my years in journalism I had grown calluses on my heart. It isn't until you find a real 'for instance' staring you in the face — something more close-up than usual, that tugs at your heart strings and resonates with the way you're personally wired — that you are touched.

I think what finally got to me that first day was a meeting with a reporter from the local Fox News TV channel. He was shaking his head after interviewing a construction worker who'd only just come out of Ground Zero after several days there.

'They were searching in a building right across the road from the World Trade Center,' he told me. 'Going through the rubble they found some things which appeared to have been blown right out of one of those aircraft that hit the buildings. Among the rubble and glass they discovered two arms bound together with some wire.'

The supposition, the reporter told me, was that these were the bound arms of one of the pilots, who'd been disabled and then, one could only hope, killed by the terrorists before the plane crashed into the tower. At about that moment, as the raw reality of what the last minutes must have been like for some of those who'd died on 11 September started to sink in, another of the sombre convoys went by.

It happened every time they found the body of a policeman or firefighter in the rubble: everything at Ground Zero would stop, hats would be removed, and the body would be carried out in a vehicle, escorted by police bikes and other emergency vehicles with lights flashing but sirens silent. My conversation with the reporter, and the sight of people standing to attention as each convoy headed uptown, began to dent my numbness just a little.

One of the challenges we were to face even on that first morning was working out what would be appropriate for a one-hour programme on New Zealand television given that our story would not go to air for another 10 days. It now being almost a week since

154

the tragedy, there had already been saturation coverage in New Zealand of just about every aspect of the attacks. What would people want to know, we wondered, when our story finally aired 15 days after the events of 11 September?

The screens back home had already featured quite a number of stories about how New Zealanders had coped, or where they'd been and what they'd seen, on the day itself. So it became a question of trying to assemble a story that both paid tribute to native New Yorkers and explored the minds of New Zealanders who had been at the heart of events — people who by now had perhaps had a chance to gather their thoughts and decide whether New York was the place where they wanted to live.

Grappling with these issues was an Auckland woman called Melissa Jenner. We met Melissa on the 45th floor of a smart Park Avenue tower, about five kilometres up the road from the World Trade Center. She had been working for a subsidiary company of the giant bonds trading corporation Cantor Fitzgerald. On the morning of 11 September she'd been running late for a meeting at the World Trade Center. Her tardiness had saved her life, and she had found herself running away from the scene of the disaster with thousands of other shocked New Yorkers.

But her firm, which had occupied many of the top floors of one of the towers, had been absolutely devastated by the attacks. Seven hundred staff at Cantor Fitzgerald had lost their lives, and on this Monday morning, part of Melissa's job was to coordinate efforts to liaise with grieving families. With little or nothing in the way of computer resources or office space, her team was shuffling between premises owned by Cantor Fitzgerald's lawyers and advertising agency. She had the look of a possum caught in the headlights of an oncoming logging truck. She hadn't slept properly for days, and was clearly postponing her personal grief until she was free to let her guard down.

Right now she was in coping mode, if only just. 'As long as I've got someone alongside me, helping me to make sane decisions, I think I might make it through today,' she told me in a fairly frazzled interview we conducted in the foyer of the lawyers' offices. 'A couple of days ago I couldn't even keep a telephone number in my head, and I think with what I'm having to do now I must be one of the most hated people around here, because I have to be tough and get on with it.'

Melissa showed me the call centre they'd set up, where phones rang constantly as relatives of Cantor Fitzgerald employees sought information, solace and help. 'Some people last five hours in here, others only five minutes,' she said in a whisper. She began leafing through a bunch of phone messages at least six centimetres thick, and in the space of the next few minutes she counselled, cajoled and tried to think creatively as multiple challenges were thrust under her nose. 'I think I'm going to go to one more large memorial service here in a week or so, and then I'll look seriously at clearing out,' she told me. 'I don't think my emotions are going to be able to stand much more than that.'

From where we stood at the window on Park Avenue, the lower part of Manhattan, away in the distance, was shrouded in a kind of mist. 'This is not the New York I came here for,' Melissa went on, 'and I don't think it's the kind of place some New Yorkers are going to want to call home when all this has settled down a bit.' She tugged constantly at the fold-over on her polo-neck sweater, and with each passing moment seemed ever closer to emotional meltdown.

'I must have run down fifty flights of stairs here more than a dozen times in the last couple of days,' she said. She and others in the building, already on a knife edge, their emotions blistered, gnawed by anxiety, were falling prey, like tens of thousands of other New Yorkers, to the near-constant barrage of false alarms and hoax bomb calls being inflicted on them by who knows what kind of warped individuals taking advantage of the fragile state of the city's nerves.

Down on the street a little later, young New York men in sharp suits and with $120 haircuts had the same glazed look in their eyes. 'This isn't the place I grew up,' one told me as he watched yet another bomb squad expert suit up in heavy clothing and prepare to go into a building to look at someone's briefcase. Another young man fairly snarled at me and glared down the barrel of the camera: 'Let's tell these people right here and now, whoever they are, "Stop hiding in your caves!" Let's get this thing on and let's get it over with!'

The traffic should have been light that morning, given there were tens of thousands who'd stayed away or been relocated, but the panic being generated by bomb alerts meant the streets of midtown Manhattan were almost in their usual state of gridlock. Negotiating side streets and short cuts in our Ford Explorer, we made our tortuous way to the offices of Saatchi & Saatchi, where we were due to meet the CEO, one-time New Zealand advertising guru Kevin Roberts.

Up till this point the closest we'd got to Ground Zero had been some distance away at street level. Now, in the Saatchi office, we had a grandstand view of the smouldering pile of rubble that had once been the twin towers. 'There were five hundred people here at these windows, with a box seat for what unfolded,' Roberts told me soberly as we gazed at a scene that looked like something out of Dresden in the Second World War.

'None of us is sleeping right now,' he went on. 'We've all got our own nightmares: for me it's great fireballs like the one I saw when the second plane hit; for my partner here, he keeps seeing the sky filled with bodies.' As we filmed, I tried to form a mental picture of what it would have been like, standing at these windows, watching what must have looked like Armageddon being unleashed upon the city in which these people had once felt so safe.

'We had major emotional breakdowns happening all around us here, right where I'm standing,' said Roberts. 'It looked like war, it smelled like war and by God it felt like war. I've been in some scary situations around the world, had guns thrust underneath my nose in all sorts of places, and I can tell you I've never felt so scared as I felt standing here six days ago.'

At such a time, I reasoned, the idea of cashing up and returning to somewhere remote and relatively safe like New Zealand must have seemed awfully tempting. Roberts nodded and thought for a moment. 'Yeah,' he said, 'but if I go into the bush somewhere, if I head for a ranch in Montana or even come back and live somewhere remote near Rotorua, then those guys win, don't they? I think our family have a bit of a rebel streak in them and we've decided to fight that kind of thinking. My kids are all heading over here shortly, a couple of them to undertake study. We're not leaving.'

Around this time, some of the things Roberts had been saying publicly about the attacks on New York, and about the implications of what had happened for the Western way of life, came in for some fairly sharp criticism in various newspaper columns, especially in New Zealand. I found this perplexing. Roberts is a very genial and relentlessly optimistic man, and the way he had pulled his own staff together and refocused their efforts after standing with them and watching the nightmare I found as inspiring as some of the things Rudy Giuliani had been commended for doing.

How easy it is to sit back at a distance and accuse someone in the middle of the unimaginable of engaging in hubris. At that time Roberts was putting in 18-hour days, spending a fair amount of time hugging and listening to staff members as they poured out tales about friends they'd lost, or lamented how their sense of composure had been shattered by what they had endured during the past week.

For a time, all three of us in our crew stood at the window and drank in the scene that lay before us a few blocks away. The Statue of Liberty seemed a small, ineffectual thing, standing out there at the end of Manhattan Island, on guard in the harbour, while a glance away was what seemed a far more potent symbol: a memorial to incredible fanaticism, determination and hatred.

Columns of trucks and earth-moving equipment were heading in and out of the area. The job of shifting one-and-a-half-million tonnes of rubble was destined to take weeks, months perhaps, above a still-blazing underground fire they said was going to burn white hot for ages.

Later that day we joined the queues outside police headquarters in downtown New York, keeping company with TV crews and journalists from a score of different nations as we waited for the accreditation that would allow us through the police lines to take a camera into the most devastated part of the city.

It was a three-hour wait in the heat, and every now and then cameras on shoulders or round necks would whir and click madly as policemen escorted the ashen-faced relatives of yet another person identified among the wreckage into the police station to complete the necessary paperwork. Here was where it started to hit home — seeing real people facing unimaginable grief.

Armed with our police passes, we trudged for kilometres through deserted streets to the Wall Street area, just round the corner from where the World Trade Center had once stood. Suddenly, there were crowds. Somehow, hundreds of people had penetrated the police cordon and were standing just a hefty stone's throw from the wreckage site. The scene of disaster, about 6.5 hectares in area, had become a tourist attraction.

Among the crowd were some highly articulate teenagers. One ran his finger along the ledge of a Wall Street building to collect some of the minute grains of dust that had been part of the solid structure of the World Trade Center towers. 'Wow,' he said quietly. 'I guess the Peter Pan syndrome has gone for us, right?'

Another said, 'Whoever thought this could happen in my neighbourhood? Where will it stop now? Some guy with explosives strapped to his body could run into my building, like over there in Jerusalem, right?'

'I guess I'm scared,' said another. 'If America ends up going to war, who's gonna be called to the battle but us young guys, and I don't want to die.'

A rabbi from the National Guard stood contemplating the scene. 'I'm going to have to give a sermon to a few of the Jewish guys in there tomorrow,' Jacob Goldstein muttered quietly as we filmed.

'What are you going to tell them?' I asked.

'Just have to tell them the best way I know how,' he said simply.

Here, for us, it was most obviously on display — that American sense of invulnerability, especially among the young, shattered forever. Not far from where we were speaking, the great bronze bust of the Wall Street bull still loomed rampant over the financial district, and someone had strategically placed a 'Wanted' poster for Osama Bin Laden on the bull's butt. Such small acts of defiance aside, one was left in no doubt that although, as the Japanese found after Pearl Harbour, a sleeping giant had been awoken, the giant had had its nose well and truly bloodied.

The sense of personal engagement I had been seeking with the scale of the tragedy was starting to make itself felt. Further uptown we came upon the fire station of Engine Company 16, where some appliances returned for no more than 90 seconds before being called out by another malicious false alarm. The death toll from this station was fairly typical of the heavy losses suffered by the New York Fire Service. On a blackboard near the front of the building, surrounded by balloons, candles and photographs, the daily roster for Ladder No. 7 had had none of the quickly scrawled chalk marks from 11 September rubbed out yet. None of the guys from that crew had come back from their last assignment at the World Trade Center. Nine men from a station of 25 firefighters were missing, presumed dead.

You looked at the roster list and were suddenly reminded what an incredible melting pot of cultures and races New York is — surnames like Richard, Princiotta, Cain, Mendez. The station that afternoon was a refuge for numbed-out people — firefighters and waiting relatives alike. The flowers and flags that choked the entrance were certainly designed to help — they came with messages aplenty from a grateful New York public — but today, six days after the attacks, hope was starting to run more than a little thin as people realised what was involved in trying to dig out fallen comrades from beneath the flattened remains of two of the world's tallest structures.

But you don't get a real handle on human resilience until you meet a firefighter's mum like Rosemary Cain. There she was, pointing out to me with great animation the photo display of her son's life, displayed prominently in the middle of the makeshift memorial under the roster sign.

'How old is George?' I asked her, as she held on tightly to my hand and gave me a steely look of determination.

'Thirty-five,' she said simply. 'He loved his job. We love coming in here because these guys give us strength. They're a wonderful, wonderful bunch of men, and they're all heroes in their own way.'

My eyes darted away and scanned the photos on the board. George, a big husky guy, was pictured in a dozen different poses with a broad grin framed by a bushy moustache. In one snapshot he was with a son in pyjamas; in another, with Mum at a camp site, in adventure ski gear ready to tackle an awesome slope.

I asked what turned out to be a presumptuous question. 'When did you get the news that George wasn't coming back?'

'I don't know that he's *not* coming back,' said Rosemary. 'I'm still hoping for a miracle, I really am. I've always believed that God was going to take care of George — I told him that constantly. He used to go out adventure skiing in wild places in Colorado for two months at a time, and I used to tell him that I worried about him more on the ski slopes than I did when he was on the fire engine.'

I thought hard for a moment. How do you ask questions at a time like this without sounding offensive, mawkish or dumb?

'So, Rosemary, what you're telling me is that somewhere under all that rubble you believe there may be a pocket of air, that George is in there and that he may still be alive and going to make it out OK?'

Before I'd even finished the question Rosemary nodded furiously and told me that was certainly what she believed.

Next morning, the traffic and blocked streets still a nightmare, we made our way through town to interview a man we'd heard had a remarkable story to tell. He was a New Zealander called Steve Domney, who originally hailed from Palmerston North, had made it big on Wall Street, and had only just escaped the disaster at the World Trade Center by a matter of moments.

On the morning of 11 September, at his home on Long Island, Steve had made an important decision — to leave late in order to see his daughter off to school. That meant his train was only just coming into a station on the Long Island side of Manhattan when the first tower was struck. 'If I hadn't decided to take those extra few moments with my daughter,' he told me as we walked up Wall Street that morning, 'I would have been in a train right underneath the World Trade Center.'

A witness to the start of the carnage through the carriage window, Steve had urged others off the train and then simply stood on the platform, his mouth gaping, watching the horrific events of the next hour or so unfold.

Now back at work, Steve looked weary and haggard as he stood with us outside 100 Wall Street and reflected on the scores of colleagues and friends he'd lost in the buildings which had once stood a couple of blocks from there.

'I've got mouth ulcers at the moment, which I *never* get,' he said. 'I'm not sleeping properly. Every day you hear a mixture of the horrific and the amazing stories about how some died and how others had almost unbelievable escapes. I find myself in serious emotional overload. How do you deal with the combination of great relief and guilt you feel over the fact that you lived and your mates died? That's what I'm grappling with.'

As we walked past National Guardsmen, and cherry pickers bearing workmen still hosing down the sides of Wall Street buildings, Steve asked me, 'Can you smell it?'

'Smell what?' I asked.

'It's kind of acrid. It's hanging in the atmosphere. The air's normally quite clear here but I can see particles all around me.'

Not only did Steve have a good tale to tell about escaping death under the World Trade Center, he was also beginning to wonder whether there wasn't someone looking after him in a cosmic kind of way. In the late 1990s he'd been spending a good deal of time looking after the affairs of a business in Geneva. Due to pay one of his regular visits to his partner there, he postponed his journey for two or three days, and was horrified when he awoke one morning to the news that the plane he'd been booked on — Swissair flight 114 — had crashed into the Atlantic.

Did all of this make him feel lucky?

'Perhaps more a little nervous and apprehensive these days,' he told us. He had invitations to more memorial services over the next few days than he could emotionally cope with. As for his long-term plans — whether to stay in New York with his young family — it was still too early to say, his nerves too raw.

'I think of myself as a relatively civilised human being,' Steve told us. 'But the one thing I can't get my head around is what these extremists did by climbing on to those planes and deliberately flying them into buildings filled with my friends. When I read the account which suggested some of the terrorists were out actually drinking and living it up a little the night before they committed these atrocities, I think to myself, what cynicism. How can you place such a low value on the lives of other people? It's such an alien concept.'

Any time you work on a story as dramatic as the aftermath of the New York terrorist attacks, you can't fail to be amazed by the

sheer resilience of some people. Over the years I've been fascinated as I've tried to figure out what it is in such individuals' pasts
that has endowed them with the ability to recover quickly from a
major setback.

I did a lot of this kind of wondering as I met a 26-year-old legal
executive, originally from Auckland, who was the one New Zealander we had known for sure had been in the World Trade Center
when the first plane had struck. Mikhaila Nola had been working
in her office on the 56th floor when the aircraft had ploughed into
the building many floors above her. Her most vivid recollection of
that morning, as I walked with her in Central Park eight days later,
was the face of a firefighter she'd seen running up the stairs towards her as she'd hurried out of the building.

'He had the most beautiful blue eyes — quite haunting, actually,' Mikhaila told me. 'I see him now as a bit of a ghostly image in
my mind, racing up the stairs to try and save lives.'

The firefighter had taken Mikhaila's hand and urged her to get
out a whole lot faster than she'd been planning.

'I have no idea what happened to that guy. I suspect that, like
so many others, there's no way that if he had kept going in the
direction he was headed he could have made it out.'

Mikhaila, however, on the day of our interview, was the very
picture of composure. She was talking calmly and analytically about
what she, her firm and the city had endured over the previous
week. Hers were the tones, recollections and ideas of a young
woman who seemed completely together, and in a mood not to be
weighed down by what she had witnessed, but to go on and never
'to be a victim'.

'We've got some new offices now, and people tell me — they
keep urging me — that I should get some counselling, but I don't
feel like I need any right now. I think in due time I'll talk about it
to my friends, people who understand, and I'll get it all out. Maybe
one day I'll feel the need to open up, but for now I'm so caught up
in the fact that I am incredibly fortunate to be alive.'

Nonetheless, Mikhaila was starting to think seriously about
heading home to New Zealand — for some time out, at least.

'I think where I most need to be right now is back with my
family. New York's been good to me, and I'd be stupid to give up

163

for ever the very good job I've got here, but I think I need to get away, to do whatever personal healing is necessary and then maybe return one day.'

Mikhaila, it appeared, had learned a lot from her mum. The photos in her apartment showed a vivacious woman who had helped thrust her into a host of challenging situations when she was relatively young — overseas travel at an early age, lots of 'in at the deep end' stuff.

After offering us lemonade and a bottle of New Zealand wine she'd kept in her fridge for a special occasion, she spoke confidently and knowledgeably about the way her firm had been set up to recover from even this, the most unthinkable of disasters.

'I mean, how does a law firm survive?' I asked her. 'With all of the premises gone, with all of your files presumably destroyed?'

'It's amazing,' she told me. 'In fact, one of my jobs recently has been coordinating something we call disaster files. The back-up system actually worked! I am so amazed that in only five working days, our entire company has been relocated. I'm not expected back at work for a couple of days, but when I go there, I'll have my office completely set up again, my own computer, probably my original phone diverted from where it used to be. I guess in this day and age it's called covering your arse, and it worked!'

As the days and nights wore on that week, we were drawn, like moths to a flame, to the night-time vigils that seemed to attract ever-increasing numbers of New Yorkers, at places like Union Square, in the heart of the city. Here, there was an outpouring of popular sentiment such as had probably not been seen since the massive antiwar demonstrations of the 1960s. Sombre statues of heroes of the War of American Independence were draped with makeshift decorations. There was a sea of American flags, and a neverending stream of people ready to stand up in front of hastily gathered crowds to sing songs, but this time celebrating the American spirit rather than pleading for peace. I wondered what Pete Seeger would have made of it all if he'd been thrust into the middle of the crowd.

This was truly where you felt the heartbeat of a great city and its wounded people. As we watched, we tried to figure out what the net outcome would be of the resolve these people seemed to be showing. Charles Krauthammer, in *Time* magazine, captured it neatly some time later:

> We had been on a holiday from history, and a well deserved one. For 50 years (1941 to 1991), America had been locked in titanic, existential struggle with Fascism, Nazism and then Communism. We won, but half a century of mobilisation can be psychologically exhausting, and we needed a rest. In the 90s, we took it. What Bin Laden did not understand, however, is that, while on vacation, America remained on call. His mistake was to place the call.

My most lasting impression? That week in New York, we saw people discovering, perhaps many of them for the first time, the art of genuine appreciation — of letting those who stood in the breach for them know how loved they were.

On our last afternoon in Manhattan, we stood outside a building on 57th Street and watched as frightened people huddled on the pavement, wondering whether this alarm was a real one or not. After a few moments, as we were about to leave, I tapped cameraman Vaughan Scott on the shoulder and said, 'Just wait, just wait.'

We were running late for our next appointment but I had a sense that something was about to unfold. Sure enough, as the firefighters emerged, there was an eruption of applause, hooting, whistling and raucous cheers. These guys, who had probably walked in and out of false alarms many times before in their professional careers, had surely never heard such thunderous acclaim. Faint smiles played across their faces. Here was genuine, unmasked appreciation, love and respect. Krauthammer, in *Time*, put it beautifully:

> We awoke with a jolt. Overnight, this land of 'Bowling Alone', of Internet introversion, of fractious multi-culturalism, developed an extraordinary solidarity — a vast outpouring of charity and volunteering; a suppression of partisanship and ethnic division; a coalescing behind resolute national leadership anchored by a new, untested president who rose extraordinarily to the occasion.

We came back to New Zealand and put our one-hour documentary to air in record time. It had been a fascinating experience — one to sharpen any journalist's interest in international affairs. A handful of men with primitive weapons had changed everyone's world, and to have played even a small part in recording that reality was enough to give back a writer his edge for a long time to come.